Soul Search

(My search for Spiritual Truth)

by

GW00458981

Geoffrey Hayward

© Geoffrey Hayward

ISBN 0-9534671-3-9

Published by
The Whole Being Centre Publications
174, Newman Road, Exeter EX4 1PQ

INDEX

FOREWARD
By Stella Blair

PREFACE

PART ONE
The Life, work and spiritual experiences of Geoffrey Hayward

PART TWO
The evidence of survival (selected accounts)

i

DEDICATION

To Mum and Dad for their help and support, To my best friends, Roy and Jane Francis also Sarah and Mitch Williams for their loyal friendship.

ACKNOWLEDGMENTS

To the many sitters who have contributed their accounts of the evidence received. Also to Psychic News and other Spiritualist publications for records of evidence. To the many Spiritualist Churches, Organisations and Societies who have supported my work over the past thirty years. In particular also to the Spiritualist Association of Great Britain who have employed me as a Medium for over twenty continuous years.

Foreword

Try and imagine the scene. It is a chill night – February 7, 1872, to be precise. See, sense and smell Victorian London. Outside, gaslights flicker in an evening breeze. Indeed, it looks as though snow might be on the way. Horses jostle for space on the ever-crowded roads, their warm breath looking like ghostly vapour. People are rushing home, everyone from the street urchins and traders to the professional classes. Even the old lady selling violets seems anxious to vacate her pitch and head for the often foul-smelling East End and her large, ever-demanding family. Women, many wearing fur mufflers and sensible hats against the increasingly bitter cold, occasionally lift their now absurdly long dresses just an inch or so to escape puddles, some of which are just starting to ice over...

Now the scene switches to 16, David Street, Marylebone in London's West End. Around a dozen friends have gathered. Perhaps they were very different in class, size, education and background: that we do not know. But what we do know is that they had but one purpose – to discuss forming a Spiritualist society. After all, modern Spiritualism had begun in America in 1848. Surely it was time to establish a Spiritualist organisation in the UK.

Perhaps seated informally around a table – the well-stacked fire occasionally belching smoke as a north wind blew down the chimney – the friends decided that, yes, they would form a society. A few meetings were arranged.

On July 10 of that same year, the Marylebone Spiritualist Association came into being as an organisation. During the early years, meetings were held at various locations throughout London, even including a carpenter's workshop and former police court. Later renamed the Spiritualist Association of Great Britain (SAGB), now we leap forward in time to 1955. It was then that a major move – literally! – occurred and the Association purchased a lease on its present premises, 33, Belgrave Square, in the heart of plush Belgravia.

True to its founding fathers, the Association is at the very forefront of promoting high-quality Mediums from all parts of the UK in addition to already established Mediums. Public demonstrations of clairvoyance are held daily so that everyone – convinced Spiritualist or not – can attend and, perhaps for the first time, come into contact with mediumship and Spiritualism.

Geoffrey Hayward has not only worked at the SAGB for over twenty years, but is senior Medium in terms of continuous service. Working away from the limelight, he is a sincere and dedicated ambassador for the spirit world. As well as serving the Association and Spiritualist churches within the UK, Geoffrey also demonstrates throughout Germany, Denmark, Austria and Switzerland, he also works in Belgium Norway and Portugal. His book is a valuable addition to literature devoted to mediumship and evidence that mankind survives physical death. It is not written by a fey mystic, but an ex-Tax executive who now deals with spirit returns!

As such, the SAGB does not have an official Mission Statement, but if it did, perhaps it would run along these lines:

"To offer evidence to the bereaved that man survives the change called death and, because he is a spiritual being, retains the faculties of individuality, personality and intelligence, and can willingly return to those left on earth, ties of love and friendship being the motivating force."

"To offer spiritual healing to those suffering from disease, whether in mind, body or spirit, in a warm and loving environment."

"With both of these objectives in mind, to offer the best and highest so that those on both sides of the veil can progress in a truly spiritual sense."

Through both public demonstrations of clairvoyance and private sittings, Geoffrey Hayward is helping us to fulfil that vital mission...

Stella Blair,

President, Spiritualist Association of Great Britain

Introduction

I have now completed thirty years work as a Medium, and as I feel it is something of a milestone I thought it an appropriate time to record some of my experiences. My psychic perception has been such a big influence in my life and I consider Spiritualism to be both my religion and my philosophy.

In recent years the public perception of psychic matters has changed. The subject has become more popular and more widely understood. Many people, from all walks of life feel no longer restricted by the straitjacket of orthodox thinking. The result of this has been a great deal of public interest in psychics and mediums who have produced or been the subject of many articles, biographies and interviews by all sections of the media. During the course of my investigations I have met many fine mediums who have been a great influence upon both my life and psychic development. It is a pity that many have not recorded their experiences and achievements. In consequence much has been lost from psychic literature. I hope through this book to inspire many as I have been inspired by those who have gone before. Not only do I hope you will be able to relate some of your life experiences to mine. I wish you to discover the spirit within you.

I hope in this book that I will add something valuable to the reader's spiritual search for truth. Evidence of that we as individuals survive death of the physical body and are able to communicate with those left on Earth has in my view been proved countless times. The old saying no one has ever been back is a false one by those not informed of the subject. For anyone on this pathway of discovery I trust that you will meet, as I have done many fellow travellers that have enriched my life.

Whilst I would never wish to force my values and opinions on to others I seek to address myself to the tremendous number of people who are anxious to find something on which to base their trust and confidence in the future. Spiritualism has a wider mission than even some Spiritualists realise.

I believe in survival after death not only because the process of evolution and the nature of life points to such a belief. There is of course considerable evidence in the form of psychic phenomena to support this hypothesis.

Today no fair-minded person who has fully studied Spiritualism and Psychical Research cannot fail but be impressed not only by the variety but the tremendous weight of evidence presented. Through the real understanding of our spiritual selves we can begin to understand the true meaning of life.

Surely also the purpose of the deeper aspects of Spiritualism is to bring about, through the understanding of its philosophy and phenomena, the desire to influence people to create a more just and sane society.

During the last thirty years not only have I witnessed practically every known Psychic gift through the mediumship of others but I have demonstrated my gifts to many tens of thousands and have taken literally thousands of public meetings and private sessions. At the SAGB and the hundreds of Spiritualist churches and centres fine work is being done by many people who seek no reward. This work gives fresh hope to the bereaved and a new meaning to life. It is to them the unsung heroes that this book is dedicated. We are indeed blessed that as Spiritualists we can continue to spread our spiritual truths without persecution. This book is also dedicated to the many that have inspired me personally on my pathway of spiritual enlightenment.

Geoffrey F Hayward

2003

PART ONE

Chapter One

Early Days

It was 1949 and times were difficult in the bleak austere years in Britain following the Second World War.

True England was at peace but the war years had changed society forever. The Labour Party had been swept to power with a huge majority in 1945 but the real post war recovery was yet to come. Mum and Dad had married in 1945 and my Sister Pat had been born the next year. Times were difficult as they were for many other young married couples in a similar position at this time. Originally from Yeovil in Somerset they had moved away from their roots to Bournemouth where my Father was employed as an engine driver on the railway.

For Mum and Dad to own their own property was only a dream as Dad's wage was relatively low so their only option was to keep moving from one rented accommodation to another. It was difficult to know how to make ends meet, however they were delighted when in the autumn of 1948 Mum found out she was pregnant. My Sister's birth had been relatively uncomplicated, so apart from an urgent review of the family's financial position my arrival was anticipated with pleasure. It came as quite a shock when serious complications arose with Mum's pregnancy. The Consultant Mr Gautier-Smith a tall slim man well respected professionally tried to be as sympathetic as possible. His final words struck home the hopelessness of the situation, "don't be too concerned, there is not a chance this baby will live you will just have to try again."

Mum and Dad returned home with heavy hearts. It was difficult to understand or accept the situation especially taking into account the lack of problems with my Sister's birth. Further discussions with the Consultant Mr Alders were equally pessimistic. So I entered this world on 18th March 1949 against all expectations. I was two and a half months premature, only two and one half pounds in weight and I had a hole in the heart. Soon after birth I developed serious breathing difficulties. The decision was immediately made, to aid my breathing, to put me into an oxygen tent. Given these factors, even taking into account the considerable advances in medical knowledge and resources, had I been born today my chances of survival would be slim. In those far off days my chances were considered as non-existent. Yet incredibly against the odds I hung on to life and refused to die. The early weeks were crucial but luckily several things were on my side. Mum and Dad's love and

1

devotion to me was such an important factor. So was my determination and will power to live. Equally important was the marvellous dedication of the nursing staff. The nurses with great compassion paid special attention to me. There was I understand even competition to nurse me.

I accept without the help and assistance of these wonderful people I would not have survived. But I also believe an additional factor made a considerable contribution. I firmly believe I had divine help from those spiritual beings on the other side. I also consider, through the circumstances of my birth lies the origin of my intuitive and mediumistic gift.

Gradually in those first few weeks in hospital I made progress although on several occasions it was touch and go. Finally after some six weeks I was allowed home. A short newspaper report appeared in the local newspaper The Evening Echo as follows:

"When baby Geoffrey Hayward came into this world last March three months before he was expected he weighed only two pounds five ounces, today he tips the scales at seven pounds eleven ounces. He has been home with his parents only a fortnight. When he was born he was fed through tubes and kept in an oxygen tent. He has done marvellously thanks to the great kindness of doctors, sisters and nurses at Boscombe Hospital his Mother told me."

The doctors at this stage wanted to send me to a special nursing clinic for premature babies. Mum and Dad with typical determination decided that loving care at home would be the best policy. The medical authorities were not pleased about this and more or less told Mum and Dad if something went wrong it would be due to their insistence on taking me home. However with the care provided at home my health gradually improved.

During the next few weeks I gained some weight although I was still pathetically small. The hole in the heart became relatively smaller and although doubts were raised as to the quality of life ahead and anxious times remained in the future the immediate crisis had been overcome, I would survive.

It is not surprising, knowing what I have come through, that I have always had a deep belief in both God and the power of prayer. Today I am over six feet in height and have the greatest difficulty in keeping my weight under fourteen stone.

So I had come through such a traumatic time. I was at that date the lightest and most premature baby born at Boscombe Hospital to have survived. Mum and Dad were certain that I was destined to do something special in my life.

The combination of my premature birth and the effect of the oxygen administered in the oxygen tent, I understand, damaged my vision beyond repair and in particular my right eye was affected by retinopathy of prematurity. The retina is the light sensitive tissue layer at the back of the eye that transmits the messages of the light rays along the optic nerve to the brain where understanding of what is seen takes place. My retinas especially the one in my right eye had become abnormal due to the stretching and distorting of scar tissue. The result of this has been limited vision in my left eye and more or less no vision in my right eye. Fairly recently I watched a programme on TV about premature babies born in the United States in the late 1940's and early 1950's. Many of them suffered from retinopathy of prematurity and completely lost all vision. I understand that Stevie Wonder, the famous American musician, comes into this category. You can therefore understand how much I have always valued my limited eyesight and been thankful for what I have.

I remember little of my first family home in the Bournemouth suburb of Boscombe literally a stone's throw from the hospital where I was born. This large typical late Victorian property was then divided into flats. My parents lived in rooms on two floors. An inconvenient arrangement, especially the transportation of prams, in those days not collapsible, groceries and suchlike up and down the stairs. The living conditions were in other ways far from ideal the rooms being particularly damp and cold in the winter.

The other tenants were mainly young married couples with children, trying to save a little to graduate to something better. At this time, just after the Second World War there was a severe housing shortage. Many were destroyed during the hostilities. In addition new building had been suspended and the post war reconstruction promised by the Labour Party was not yet in full swing.

So Mum and Dad with their young family in common with many thousands struggled on as best they could. The private landlords in a position of strength in these times took a 'take it or leave it' attitude. Hard as times were at least conditions socially were better than at the end of the First World War when the returning troops had been promised a land fit for heroes. My parents had vivid memories, I am sure all their generation have, of ex-servicemen with terrible injuries, standing on street corners, perhaps selling matches, or playing a harmonica, trying to earn some sort of living. During those times life was incredibly hard due to mass unemployment and a lack of social security. At least Dad had a regular job and a regular income even though by today's standards life was grim.

In 1952 Mum and Dad were offered, owing to much persistence by Mum who was a frequent visitor to the council housing department, a brand new three bedroom house on one of the many new council estates then being built on the outskirts of Bournemouth. This meant a considerable improvement to the cramped conditions of their flat. Mum was particularly pleased that she would have her own kitchen instead of sharing one. There were other considerable advantages, the estate was nicely situated, and our house had a large garden for Pat and I to play in, overlooked at the back by allotments and the countryside surrounding the villages of Holdenhurst and

Throop. This was especially good for Dad, as well as being a countryman at heart; he was a keen gardener. It was also felt the environment would be beneficial to my health, I was still delicate to say the least and particularly prone to chest infections.

So as our family made preparations for the move a new era was beginning. Our new family home would not only embrace my whole childhood, with many wonderful adventures, but would see, although I did not understand it at the time, the awakening of my psychic gifts.

Twenty-five years later I decided, to leave my family home, I bought a flat in the very same road as the home we were now moving from, one of the many coincidences that have happened in my life

Chapter Two

Childhood

My progress as a toddler was very slow. Amazingly I was two and a half years old before I was able to walk. For a while I could walk just holding Mum or Dad's hand but I just did not have the confidence to walk unaided. I well remember the time I first walked alone.

We were spending our holidays at Auntie Dolly's caravan park at Weymouth Dorset. Showing my usual lack of confidence I was walking holding on to a wire fence. My Father suddenly rather sharply shouted " come to Daddy " this seemed to do the trick and I walked to him without help. I still have photographs of me by that wire fence the scene of my triumph.

I have always liked my name although I don't like the American version Jeff. Dad has always been fond of boxing and horseracing. During the course of his interest he was in contact with a well known newspaper racing columnist named Geoffrey Gilby who showed my Father considerable kindness. In fact at one time he sent Dad two tickets for one of Randolph Turpin's important fights held at a packed Wembley Stadium in 1948. Needless to say tickets for this event were very hard to obtain. In time Dad lost contact with him but never forgot his kindness, so I was named in memory of this fine gentleman. Nowadays there is an annual race 'the Geoffrey Gilby Memorial Handicap Chase' that usually attracts a good class field. So it is nice that the racing fraternity still honour this gentleman. I understand he left this life many years ago.

The choosing of my middle name Frederick was a little more conventional as I was named after my paternal Grandfather who had died at an early age. Dad had always been conscious how much he had missed out from his Father's early death and was always determined to be a strong influence upon his children. My parents had been brought up in Yeovil in the 1920's and 1930's. During this period the town was famous for the gloving industry. Unfortunately the workers in this industry had worked under appalling conditions. Tuberculosis or TB was rife at this time the disease carried off whole families a timely reminder of how social conditions have improved in the lifetimes of many. For some reason the workers in this industry seemed to be especially prone to this disease, my Grandfather on Father's side was in this trade for a number of years and was one such victim.

The family liked our new surroundings situated so near to the countryside. However the house was really cold especially in the winter. These days were before central heating and fitted carpets. Due to my delicate constitution I spent many hours

5

in bed with coughs and colds. I now started to experience my first psychic contacts, being frequently aware of an elderly lady by my bed. I felt her presence warm and comforting.

My parents took her to be simply an imaginary figure, looking back the experience of seeing this lady was so real to me. She seemed to draw close to me especially when I was in distress or needed comfort. I can picture her now clearly so vivid are these experiences of long ago. She had grey hair neatly tied back and was neat and slim in build. But it was the wonderfully kind radiance that made such a big impression. It is only in discussion with my family in recent times that have established the description of the lady corresponds closely to my Father's Grandmother. Apparently she had a great love of children and was highly respected. Although I have never received specific confirmation from the spiritual world as to the identity of my spiritual visitor I feel certain now that is who I saw. In any case it was nice my first visions of this kind left me feeling warm and protected. I certainly owe this lady a dept of gratitude for her assistance at this most critical time. The memory of her special love and interest in my welfare remained an inspiration in the challenges that lay ahead that yes I was in some way protected. Even at this early stage although I obviously did not understand the implications I felt that I had a spiritual destiny. Even today the memory of my spiritual visitor fills me with a motivating power. Remembering this time was one of great stress and uncertainty. It seems that with people of psychic perception a crises often stimulates that faculty lying dormant within them. This is obviously what happened to me and explains the strong effect these frequent visitations and her exceptional spirituality had on me at the time.

People often ask me whether mediums are born or can be made. Like many questions there is no hard and fast answer. In my opinion my gifts are inherited but could have lain inactive within my sub conscious for many years. I understand that this awakening was activated by both the circumstances of my birth and my subsequent ill health that resulted in me going deeply within my own psyche. Every human being has some psychic awareness just as everyone has some artistic talent. Ability in art can range between drawing a straight line to painting a masterpiece.

Some sincere Spiritualists can sit for many years in a psychic development circle and see little or nothing. Whilst others do not really have to sit for development for the gift is in great abundance. Psychic perception in a very young child is of course more common than many believe. Due to the false materialist assumptions of our modern society our psychic gifts are pushed further and further within our sub conscious. Many early psychic impressions are merely dismissed as childish imagination.

I had a number of other psychic experiences as a boy that I generally kept quiet about. However I was lucky that my parents realised that perhaps their delicate son had an unusual sensitivity and were sympathetic to this part of me. Although Mum

6

and Dad did not at this time have any knowledge of Mediumship and Spiritualism I never remember them trying to suppress these impressions. Although my spiritual visualisation of my elderly lady were so strong and made a far greater impact than my other visions I do not consciously remember the time I stopped seeing her. It is often the way of the spirit that when a real danger period has passed they move into the background. I feel sure that in my sub conscious self I realised and accepted this and felt comfortable about it. My vision of her was so real and tangible. Many of the other experiences I had at this stage were more in the way of strong mental impressions that were too powerful to ignore. I did however in my own way try to suppress and dismiss from my conscious much of what I felt or saw.

At this time Christmas was a magical time. I was naturally extremely close to my parents. How I remember the excitement when Dad bought the Christmas tree home. One particular year the tree was so tall Dad had to cut the tree at the top to get it into the lounge. Even then it reached up to the ceiling. Just before this Christmas I was playing in the lounge with Dad when suddenly I felt very ill and collapsed. My breathing became very laboured and the doctor was urgently called, he was a G P of his time treated with much respect in our neighbourhood. Ever since I can remember I feel or obtained strong impressions around people. Some people I feel comfortable with whilst others I want to avoid. Luckily I always felt encouraged and confident in his ability to help me during my moments of need.

Dr Crawford soon diagnosed a severe bout of pneumonia and all over the Christmas period I was really poorly. I was confined to bed for the rest of the festive season but as a special treat I was brought down for a few minutes on Christmas Day. I still remember to this day being carried downstairs by Dad, yet I must have been only three or four.

7

Chapter Three

Growing Up

Finally the big day arrived and it was time to start school. In those days there were few nursery schools, instead you were harshly acquainted into a new era of life. Mum brought me to Summerbee Infants School. After being shown my new classroom and surroundings I was introduced to my teacher Mrs Scott who I thought must be very old, as she had grey hair! Mum then quietly left me so I found myself in a rather strange and hostile environment.

I soon found myself seated at a desk in the middle of three rows. On my left a little boy was crying. I then directed my vision to my right a small blonde haired girl also in tears. I found this situation very difficult to deal with. You can imagine being a sensitive lad; it was bad enough coping with my new predicament, let alone being aware of the distress around me. At such times in my life even at this early age I have been able to call upon an inner strength to deal with critical moments. Somehow I just managed to hold back the tears some achievement given the circumstances. I decided after my first day in class one that I quite liked school.

I am always thankful I was brought up in the rather unrefined atmosphere of a 1950's council estate. Many of the problems that exist today such as wanton destruction, joy riders and drugs were either rare or non-existent at this time. Not that I am suggesting these problems are just associated with housing estates. Fortunately in our road there were many children in my age group. The green area in front of our house was either Dean Court, ground of the town football club in the winter or in the summer Dean Park, ground of Hampshire County Cricket club.

Sunday was always special, a day apart and if Dad was not working the family would have walks into the neighbouring countryside. Being always a countryman at heart I think he enjoyed these outings more than anyone did. I have to admit I was always happier on the homeward journey.

My time at infants school past pleasantly. The headmistress was an elderly lady called Miss Drake, her grey hair was tied back and I worked out she must be very old indeed as she walked with the aid of a stick. She had been at the school for more years than anyone could remember and remained there some years after I left. She took a kindly benevolent view of her pupils and was very well respected.

I made the transition from infant to junior school easy enough although the change was not great as the schools adjoined each other. I did not find my lessons easy and struggled partly because of my vision difficulties and partly by reason that with various ailments I was so often off school.

At this time one of my greatest pleasures was to listen to Dad telling me of his adventures when he was a boy. I spent many magical hours hearing about his carefree country childhood. How I enjoyed hearing the same stories over and over again with fascination. What delightful interest I took, it was almost like Dad held me under a spell speaking of days and adventures that seemed so long ago. When we are children time moves so slowly. My early days were spent of course without television. I wonder whether in these more sophisticated times, in the age of videos and computer games the modern Father takes the time and trouble to communicate in this way. Certainly I doubt whether many modern children would enjoy the magical influence of storytelling as much as I did.

My growing-up days were full of occasions, Christmas and Firework Night were always thoroughly enjoyed. I well remember 'the rag and bone man' with his horse and cart and ' the French onion men ' with their bicycles and berets. My best friends were Dennis Harvey who excelled at all sports and David Stainer who was quite academic. I suppose I was a little overawed as a youngster. How I wished to be good at sport, I particularly adored football and cricket. Yet I had my own abilities, my good memory specifically being useful with my favourite subjects of history and geography. My passion for history was such that at the age of nine I could recite in order from memory the dates of the reigns of each monarch from William the Conqueror (1066-1087) to our present Queen.

Right from an early age certain people I have been in contact with give me a strong sensation of well-being whilst others have made me feel very uncomfortable. Through my make-up as an individual this intuition has always been a very strong part of me. I appreciate that everyone has these feelings to some extent. It's not explained just by physical appearance but goes beyond this. I now know that for years I have unconsciously been able to read the aura (atmosphere) around people accurately. In later years I sought to develop this to a high standard. An example of this was my relationship with Jimmy Richardson the boy living next-door. It's true he was a rough tough boy fairly uncontrollable and completely the opposite of me in practically every way. In later years I was to suffer badly with certain bullies that affected me deeply. However I never had the slightest problem in this respect from Jimmy. He was exceptionally strong and had the power to make my life miserable, yet perhaps he picked up from my aura certain gentle vibrations. Although I have not seen him for many years I understand he is a successful roofing contractor, a line of work his physique would be ideally suited to. Anyway I wish him well whatever position in life he is in.

My Sister Pat, like most young girls, was and still is crazy about all animals. One day she found a stray kitten in our garden. She pleaded with Mum and Dad to keep this kitten soon named 'Blackie'. After enquiries within the neighbourhood that failed to find his owners ' Blackie' became a valued member of our family to join Bimbo Stainer, Snowy Gillette, and Rover Shearing as pets in our road. Soon after Blackie became a permanent part of our household every summer he developed an abscess on his chest. With each year that passed the abscess became worse and worse aggravated by him scratching the affected part. Finally the situation became so bad the decision was made that it would be kinder to put Blackie to sleep. I think the cat must have heard this warning for from that moment on he made an improvement until the problem completely disappeared. I am sure that animals have a strong intuition and our cat healed himself.

I was still having great problems with my vision. Mr Whitwell, my eye specialist, was charming and put me at ease. After several consultations it was decided my right eye with negligible vision was a 'lazy' eye. To bring on any sight lying dormant my good eye was covered with a patch. The result was that I spent two troublesome months trying to find my way around using only my right eye. By all accounts I dealt with this using great patience. Perhaps I was using the same qualities that in later years enabled me to develop my psychic abilities. Although I persevered with the patch it did not bring any improvement; the experiment was therefore discontinued.

There were further problems, I had a bad squint and after some deliberation particularly taking into account various other complications the decision was made to operate. These were very anxious times and Dad especially was very concerned about the position. In fact I thoroughly enjoyed the adventure of being in hospital, the nurses were wonderful and the surgery was successful much to everyone's relief. I am convinced all these experiences were so important in developing my sensitivity in the future.

At this stage of my life I was so aware I was somehow different to most people. I was so often the looker-on given to contemplation and introspection. Luckily I had great understanding from my parents and my Sister who was very protective towards her little brother. One day when a friend of hers made some unkind comments that were about me her immediate reaction was to have nothing more to do with her, such was family loyalty.

In 1956 the local football club the then rather grandly named Bournemouth and Boscombe Athletic (later renamed AFC Bournemouth) caused rather a sensation in the FA Cup. The club belonged to the Third Division (South) and had safely negotiated the first three rounds of the Cup. For the fourth round they were drawn against Wolverhampton Wanderers at that time one of the best teams in the whole of the football league.

In our house as usual the time leading up to Christmas was exciting. Mum was making a Christmas cake and I was told to make a secret wish whilst stirring the cake mix and this wish may come true. I accordingly made the secret wish that Bournemouth would win the FA Cup. When Bournemouth travelled to the famous Molineux ground at Wolverhampton it was considered the Midlands club would win easily. The Wolves contained many famous players in their team including Billy Wright captain of England who was to go on to win over 100 international caps. The match was sensational the only goal of the day being scored by Reg Cutler the speedy Bournemouth winger. The whole town went wild with excitement and eagerly awaited the fifth round draw. Soon we heard that our team had been drawn against Tottenham Hotspur then lying second in the top Division. Bournemouth played brilliantly beating the Spurs 3-1.

Everyone suddenly realised that Bournemouth were now only two games from an appearance in the final at Wembley stadium. The result of the draw was a sixth round tie with the most famous club of all Manchester United the famous 'Busby Babes'. This team was top of the league and we all awaited the match with great anticipation. Unfortunately I was considered far too young to go to the match; the ground would be full to capacity and obtaining a ticket extremely difficult. My introduction to our local team would be a reserve game the following season. However Dad had managed to obtain a ticket and I well remember listening to the match on the radio. I was especially excited, as my secret wish for Bournemouth to win the cup appeared to be coming true. I knew that I must not tell anyone about this. Everything seemed to be working out our heroes soon took a 1-0 lead. Imagine my disillusionment when two quick Manchester United goals ended my, and many other people's, dream of our small team winning the Cup.

Soon after as a treat we were taken to London for the day. During our visit we visited a café and I was really fascinated by an Indian gentleman in a turban. I don't think there were any Indians living in Bournemouth at the time! After our meal Dad put a sixpence under a saucer as a tip for the waitress, what a marvellous man my Dad was I thought. Walking along by the Thames seeing some old coal barges go by I announced to the family "Indian War Canoes" much to everyone's amusement.

I had not as a young child given much thought to the subject of death. When we are young death seems so very far in the distance. In reality I had been, as you know, very close to death, although at this tender age I had no idea how close. Soon my cosy little world was going to be shattered.

Grandma and Granddad (Mum's parents) lived in Yeovil and a visit to them was quite an adventure because it meant a train journey of some distance. Granddad was short in stature and had a determined character. An engineer by trade he was highly respected by all who came into contact with him. Grandma was quiet, gentle and extremely placid and easy going. In a generation where women were expected to repair and make good she was very gifted at dressmaking, sewing and allied activities.

At the outbreak of war in 1914 Granddad had joined the army and fought the first battles of that terrible conflict. He was therefore an original 'Old Contemptible' so named by the German Kaiser who had initially no respect for the small British army. The ordinary German soldier soon revised this opinion, when facing the British army at Mons in Belgium. Granddad took part in this battle, for this he was awarded 'the Mons Star', a medal still treasured by the family. The so-called story of the angel of Mons alas belongs to romantic fiction rather than reality. Soon after this he was recalled to 'Civvy Street' as his ability as an engineer was considered more valuable to the war effort.

In the late 1950's regretfully Granddad developed lung cancer, an illness he faced with great courage. I well remember seeing him in bed and being presented with a watch. Even then there was a special commanding aura of respect and quality around him that impressed me greatly.

It was a cold winter's day and I was seated in our kitchen. The heating came from a rather smelly paraffin heater. Dad then told me that Grandma was coming to live with us. This news made me really happy as I thought how nice it would be to have her with us. Then I thought for a moment and then asked was Granddad also coming to stay. My Father's words really hit me when I was told Granddad had died. From one moment of happiness I had descended to great sadness. How could this be I asked myself, I had not thought that Granddad would die even though I was aware he was very ill.

Since my involvement with Spiritualism Granddad has rarely communicated through mediums. A very practical down to earth man he had at least one really strong psychic experience. His Father was very seriously ill and Granddad had just visited him. On the journey home he decided to break his journey and drove the car into a lay-by. There, whilst he was sat relaxing, the car door suddenly opened without logical explanation. This occurred at about the time that his Father actually passed over and apparently completely unnerved Granddad considerably.

So Grandma came to live with us, Mum hiding her grief very well, missed her Father so much. Its quite ironic that I have received so little proof from others of Granddad's presence yet I believe it was him that orchestrated psychic events that were to make a big impression upon me.

Grandma moved in with us and I look back with pleasure that we made her time with us as happy as possible. Unfortunately when Granddad died part of her spirit died also. As soon as Grandma moved in I became aware at night of a figure in my bedroom. At first my reaction was to dive under the bedclothes. After a while I got used to this figure in my room. The whole situation puzzled me. Often the form

12

would appear four or five times a week. Finally I decided to tell this presence that I did not want this disturbance at night. So for several evenings I told the figure in no uncertain terms to go away. On mentioning the matter to Mum she dismissed it the explanation being the person was her coming in to check I was settled for the night. I could of course not accept this account. Had I used the words to Mum spoken to the presence I would have been in trouble. The whole episode left me struggling for a meaning for what had happened. Strangely I do not remember the end result presumably the appearances got less frequent and finally ceased completely.

On reflection I am convinced that the impressions were so natural, so strong they were not due to imagination but were psychic in origin. Although I am still many years later waiting for confirmation from the Spiritual World I am convinced Granddad was behind the visitation.

Grandma only lived with us for about 18 months. Throughout her health was failing although she rarely complained. By the time she died she was very tired and I think it was a happy release from her suffering. Since her passing she has communicated several times very strongly much to my joy because of the special bond between us.

Pat, my sister was always very bright. At junior school she was in the top class and it was no surprise when she passed the 11+ examination and went to the local grammar school. She was then immediately accepted into the top stream, a first class achievement.

The day finally arrived when it was my turn to take this important examination that would determine my educational future. As I was in the fourth stream of six I was not expected to pass and in due course found myself with most of my classmates at Summerbee Secondary Modern. It was a sad farewell to junior school, as I had been happy there. I also said goodbye to my best friend Stephen Hornsby who was going to another school in the town. We subsequently lost touch and it was many years later we met again when I was taking a Spiritualist meeting.

Life at secondary school was rather a rude awakening from the rather protected environment of junior school. On our first day we were as newcomers indoctrinated into various rituals including 'the bumps'. The fourth and fifth formers seemed really big and strong. In the first few days we were subjected to quite a lot of bullying, luckily at this time my 'guardian angel' must have been with me and I escaped the worst rigours of this. Our first few days of settling in consisted of taking quite a number of examinations to assess our abilities. When the results were announced I found myself in the 'b' stream one or even two classes above most of my former classmates from junior school. It was a significant move forward leading to new challenges ahead.

I found the members of my new class a mix of personalities, some were friendly and immediately made me feel at ease, a few made me feel most uneasy and one or two I sensed clearly resented my presence. At this time my strong intuitional faculties were developing although I did not realise this. I now understand that my chakras or psychic centres were beginning to develop. These in later life I would develop, understand and use positively but all this lay far in the future. For now I wanted to belong and not to be so sensitive. Sometimes I would get a terribly uncomfortable feeling at the base of my tummy. Most people experience this before an examination, operation or similar traumatic event. Regretfully I experienced this nausea practically every day, certainly it became an unwelcome and oft repeated episode at this stage of my life. Let me explain that the Solar Plexus situated in this region is considered the most sensitive and tender of the chakras or energy centres. Not surprisingly for a number of reasons the next couple of years were rather difficult. In some subjects particularly woodwork, metalwork and mathematics I was always near or at the bottom of the class. This was especially worrying since most of the boys in the class were expected to learn a trade on leaving school. However at other subjects particularly history, geography and religious instruction I excelled always being near or at the top. This in itself set me rather apart from most of my classmates who thought it unusual to take an interest in such matters.

In my good subjects I showed a great eagerness to please whilst in the areas where I struggled I gained the reputation of being a great trier. In fact for three years running I gained the annual form prize for 'effort'. I considered this award almost my annual property such was my determination to succeed.

Although my ability was very limited I was still as crazy about sport as ever. Mr Forder, the Sports Master was kindness itself and recognised as well as my lack of ability my enthusiasm. So when I was selected to play in the school trial football match I was thrilled to be given an opportunity. The big day of the match arrived, and I was determined to give a good account of myself. A few weeks earlier I had acquired a new pair of football boots costing the grand sum of nine shillings and sixpence. How could I fail in my venture? During the match I took my usual position at right fullback and had the job of marking an exceptionally speedy winger, a boy in my own class named Peter Wells. Since speed was never my strong point I found myself struggling against my talented opponent who was considered an almost certainty for the 'a' team. Although I was beaten on several occasions our 'b' team only lost 1-0 the goal originating from the other wing I felt therefore I had done enough for selection. Alas illusions are soon shattered and when the team selection was made I was not even included as a travelling reserve to play Stourfield School. I came home with a heavy heart and in the solitude of my bedroom 'cried my heart out'.

Of course Dad and Mum were as always very sympathetic to my situation. It was fairly obvious that I was not going to earn my living as a professional footballer not the high earning profession it is today. Soon there was to be the school 'house'

14

football tournament. We had four school 'houses' divided up as York (yellow) Durham (green), Winchester (red) and my house Canterbury (blue). Due mainly to a shortage of players I was accepted to play for my house. Miracles sometimes do happen; our schoolhouse actually won the championship that year, being a member of that team was my best sporting achievement to date.

Around this time a somewhat more important championship was being won. Hampshire County Cricket Club, who I supported, won the County Championship for the first time. Throughout the 1950's Surrey had won 7 consecutive titles. However under the inspired and cavalier leadership of the captain Colin Ingleby-Mackenzie Hampshire after 66 years of trying finally won the title. I well remember the quick scoring batsman Roy Marshall, reliable Henry Horton, medium-pace bowler Derek Shackleton and the fast bowler 'Butch' White all my boyhood heroes. For years the annual Hants v Somerset fixture, often played at Dean Park Bourne-mouth was the subject of gentle rivalry between Dad and I. My individual cricket record on the local green was usually being bowled for a low score although in one match going in last I actually made 34!

At home we acquired our first black and white television in 1957. I got so much pleasure watching especially the sport. The FA Cup Final gave great pleasure, as did the Grand National. For the Boat Race the whole family with variable degrees of enthusiasm supported Oxford, regretfully during this period Cambridge usually won.

My political views were starting to develop; the house was always one of full discussion. Mum and Dad were Labour supporters through and through. Mum shopped regularly at the Co-op usually a sure sign of Socialist sympathies whilst Dad was a keen trade unionist. In the dim and distant past some of the family had actually voted Liberal. It was pointed out this was before Labour were strong. Throughout most of the 1950's and until 1964 the Tories were in power. Harold Macmillan the Prime Minister telling us "you have never had it so good" was not a popular figure in our house. So I was brought up in a two party system. Then in 1962 the Liberal party shocked the nation and themselves I suspect and won a sensational by-election victory at Orpington, Eric Lubbock the Liberal candidate overturning a huge Tory majority in what was considered a safe Tory seat. Now the Labour and Conservatives faced a positive third force in British politics.

I well remember watching the General Election results in 1964, although I followed the family tradition of supporting Labour I was impressed by the likeable Jo Grimond leader of the Liberals. It was the early awakening of a lifetime's interest in politics. That year the Labour party won a narrow victory, the Liberals made modest gains and I continued my studies.

I reached a stage that I wanted to earn some money of my own to supplement my pocket money. So I gained employment with 'Mannings Newsagent' as a paperboy delivering Evening Echo's for the grand sum of six shillings and sixpence a week (exactly one shilling and a penny a night). I certainly learned the value of money from this work. Later I obtained a " Sunday round" earning the grand sum of six shillings a day. How I hated the Sunday supplements then coming into fashion. It was very hard work delivering in all weathers.

My interest in astronomy started, my first telescope a small refractor gave great satisfaction. How I marvelled at looking at the craters on the moon and the satellites of Jupiter. Later I graduated to a wonderful three inch Victorian brass refractor. A refracting telescope uses lenses whilst many astronomical telescopes, using mirrors, are called reflectors. This was bought for fifty two pounds and ten shillings saved from many weeks paper-round money and extra earnings doing a variety of odd jobs including selling Dad's produce from the allotment door to door. The telescope was purchased in London, the salesman I remember having a special liking for whisky (although in fairness we saw him directly after lunch). Anyway it meant carrying a large tripod and telescope through the rush hour on the underground. How the three of us managed it I don't know, perhaps a case of divine help especially for Dad struggling down the escalator.

Pat, my Sister, now left school and joined the Inland Revenue as a Tax Officer the basic requirement being five G C Es at ordinary level. Dad and Mum had similar ambition for me only the main target being more modest was to get me into the Civil Service to the basic grade of Clerical Assistant. The first step was therefore an interview with firstly the kindly but authoritarian headmaster Mr A W Legg and then the Youth Employment Officer.

Mr Legg explained that I always tried my very best, I was not a practical minded lad and although I showed real ability in some subjects there was still much work to be done if I was to pursue an academic career.

At this time the minimum requirements to enter the Civil Service was two G C E's at ordinary level. The Youth Employment Officer was not an easy man to talk to. When Dad spoke of his aspirations for me the official was not very encouraging. In fact he was rather contemptuous of the idea I could attain this position. Such ambition was beyond expectations that was the indication given. His words were given a mixed reaction but Dad in particular thought I had the ability to win through in the end.

The time that I write of was not an easy period of my life. My health difficulties continued to hamper my progress. The coughs and colds I got kept me off school for weeks and weeks. My vision difficulties held me back considerably and my confidence was not helped by the bullying I encountered. Through these experiences I went deeper and deeper within myself. I am convinced now of course that these events strengthened my psyche or inner self in preparation for my spiritual work ahead. To work as a Medium effectively one needs understanding and compassion. These occurrences gave me in later life a mutual understanding with the lonely, the

16

weak and the oppressed. How can we understand the sufferings of others if we have not been subjected to similar feelings?

Let me explain why I was so vulnerable to the bullies who made my life such a misery at this time. It goes beyond mere physical appearance. As a psychic I was able, even at this time, to perceive how much more sensitive I was to the majority around me. But I also in many ways telegraphed these feelings to my associates and colleagues. In a sub conscious way all those in my proximity picked up these sensations. Obviously some reacted in a protective, sympathetic and supporting role to the vibrations around me. Others perhaps the majority acted generally in a fairly neutral way. A few, those of low spirituality and basic instincts acted in a hostile violent way, in a sense the only action they could take given their low morale development and code of conduct. So even the most basic person is capable of giving off or receiving psychic vibrations. Obviously the psychic, whether his abilities are latent or developed, is more open to these feelings whether friendly or hostile. In this particular case we can clearly see the negative vibrations given off by my oppressors and my ignorance of how to use my sensitivity in a positive way fed off each other much to my misfortune.

I cannot say I have compassion towards those who so enjoyed persecuting me the memory of which has stayed with me down the years. When I hear of other children suffering in this way my heart and soul goes out to them. In such situations you can feel utterly and desperately alone. I often think now I should have dealt with the position differently. However all things considered it's best to just endure it and trust that in time events will change for the better. I must add that I was not the only one in my class to suffer in this way. I do believe that often the perpetrators of such actions never realise the psychological harm they do. My worse tormentor has ended up very successfully in the engineering profession although others involved have I understand fallen upon difficult times. I wonder whether any had any comprehension of their actions, I would like to think yes.

Obviously there were lighter moments and I was always surrounded in the home with love and affection. We had tremendous fun at school playing up certain teachers. At one time making paper aeroplanes was in fashion. At another aircraft spotting, another improvised table tennis, using desks as a table tennis table. The whole year had competitions and to my delight and surprise I actually won my fair share of games.

Then there was the 'smokers union' that met behind the bicycle shed at break-time. One day they were caught and to everyone's amusement at next Assembly a long list of boy's names was read out to see the headmaster in his study afterwards for obvious reasons. This was followed by a solitary girl's name. This girl had quite a reputation having been expelled from the grammar school. The implications were obvious, but on this occasion not deserved. It was found out afterwards that she had to see the Head about a separate incident completely unrelated to the thirty or so boys. We liked to play practical jokes on anyone in authority. Luckily most of our adventures caused no real harm to anyone.

In 1965 Mum and Dad decided to buy a property so they began the exciting but somewhat frustrating job of 'house hunting '. I did not want to leave my boyhood home and my friends (although in truth I had grown away from most of them). I have always disliked change in my life and felt a little insecure about my future. Mum and Dad became disillusioned with their search; the state of some of the properties within their price range left a lot to be desired. One day outside yet another bungalow being viewed I just KNEW my parents would buy it. I was left in the car outside whilst they went in to inspect the interior. When they came out both were very unimpressed especially with the décor. On the journey home I was totally convinced that my strong impressions were correct. So many times over the years I have learned to listen to these feelings and to trust them. A few weeks later Mum and Dad despite initial reservations bought this bungalow partly with money left by Grandmother.

Leaving my childhood home was truly the end of an era. How we all accumulate so many things down the years. Out went so many old toys either thrown out or given away. The children down the road must have thought Christmas had come early that year. My boyhood was now behind me.

Chapter Four

Early Adulthood

After our move the pressure upon me to obtain certain qualifications increased. Our year was the first to take a new examination, the Certificate of Secondary Education. No one was quite sure of the quality needed, however it was stressed that a grade one marking would be recognised by employers as equivalent to an ordinary G C E ordinary level pass. There was much talk in our household of the success needed that would enable me to stay on to the sixth form.

Luckily the standard required was not high and I obtained passes in all five subjects I took enabling me to stay on for another year to obtain higher qualifications. Happily the bullying element had left school in 1965 and my fellow sixth form colleagues were generally a good bunch. My sensitivity was still as strong as ever but the next year was to be a fairly happy one.

About this time I first became interested in Spiritualism. The fashion at school and youth club was to have glass and alphabet séances hardly conducted in the way responsible Spiritualists would approve of. In fact generally in the middle of the Sixties there was an awakening of interest in the spiritual, the so-called 'Age of

Aquarius'. A well known toy manufacturer even made a Ouija board (marked with the alphabet and various signs used in communication with the spiritual world.) The Spiritualist movement forever aware of the dangers of uncontrolled contact with the other side mounted a successful campaign to ban the sale of such items in toyshops in Great Britain. All this did not concern me at the time and a sixth sense kept me away from any direct involvement with these activities. However during the course of the usual 'mumbo-jumbo' it was strongly rumoured that the deceased brother of a pupil had managed to communicate in one of the sessions held at this time.

One incident does stand out in the memory. Again I was not directly involved. During youth club days a particularly memorable so called glass and alphabet séance took place. At first the atmosphere in the room was jocular as various people asked certain questions. As everyone present were teenagers such questions as who will I marry and how many children will I have were asked. However as the evening progressed the atmosphere in the room changed decidedly. More detailed questions the answers of which could be verified were asked. Looking back the replies being given were fairly impressive. Unless someone with an excellent knowledge of everyone present {that I consider unlikely} was purposely pushing the glass certainly some psychic contact was being made. Whether this was merely telepathic between those present, or with an outside source it was difficult to tell. Although I was completely separate from the group in another part of a fairly large room I felt very uneasy with the proceedings. The feeling of tension filled the air. Everyone in the room was feeling this and in order to attempt to take control certain individuals tried to create the fun atmosphere that existed before the session began. This was done partly by ridiculing the actions of those holding the so-called séance. In this electrically charged situation the "spirit" purporting to communicate had a final message for each of us. This was that there would be a nuclear war the following February that would wipe out all life on Earth. Given the accuracy of what had gone on before the result was that pandemonium broke out, several of the girls breaking down in tears. In the cold light of day it is easy many years later to come to the conclusion that the results and reactions were due to a group of over imaginative teenagers. Remember that at this time the threat of nuclear war was still real between the two super powers. What I do know now three decades and more after the event is that all psychic contact has to be attempted with respect and dignity. The power of prayer is of supreme importance. I also know that like attracts like, so it is conceivable that on this occasion some joker on the other side made contact. Firstly lulling those present with a false feeling of security by giving correct answers before dropping the bombshell at the end. I cannot stress enough that those that dabble in this way can bring big trouble to themselves so DON'T DO IT under any circumstances. If you wish to make contact sit in a developing circle run by responsible Spiritualists or sit with an experienced and suitably qualified medium.

I cannot say I was pushed too hard during my last year at school. Father in particular impressed upon me the importance of obtaining English language and one other subject at G C E to obtain the target of a place in the Civil Service. I was at

19

this stage still madly keen on history and encouraged by my history master, Mr McCarthy, I was considered more or less a certainty to pass in this subject with ease. However in some of my other subjects the time that I had lost over the years with health problems started to have an affect. I still entered the examinations, the most important of my life with a measure of optimism. The endorsement coming from my teachers being I deserved to succeed.

Now came the important time of going for interviews and I soon found myself face to face with Mr Rogers Chief Collector of Taxes. During the meeting I caused some amusement by asking about the pension rights, which must have given the correct impression, as shortly afterwards I was offered a position as a temporary Clerical Assistant with the Inland Revenue. A permanent appointment would be considered on the results of my G C E's. It seemed that the dream of entering the Civil Service would be fulfilled as I proudly took up my temporary position in, by coincidence, the same office that my Sister was working as a Tax Officer.

Sometimes in life everything seems to go smoothly then comes one almighty upset. My life and my confidence were about to be tested. The day came when my examination results arrived on the doormat. Opening this with anticipation I found as expected I had passed history with ease, obtaining as it turned out, the second highest grade in the school. The highest grade being achieved by someone who had failed the exam the previous year. Of the other subjects I narrowly failed two, including my second favourite geography and failed two others by a wider margin. My whole future was now in jeopardy and the position with my job uncertain. Luckily I had settled into my work well, doing a lot of filing work that everyone else seemed reluctant to do. Apart from one most unpleasant person in authority, who I ttried to avoid, I got on quite well with the majority of my colleagues. Very nervously I saw one of the Management Inspectors and told him of my poor results. I had got myself so worked up thinking my career had ended before it had begun. Mr Dale, a tall studious looking man in his late forties, was not unsympathetic to my situation. He explained to be a permanent member of staff I could take the internal Civil Service exam and that he would discuss the situation with the other Inspector to do with staffing, Mr Scattergood.

I returned back to my desk determined that I would succeed. In those days the Civil Service was very formal. Everyone addressed those of a higher grade as Mr or Mrs or Miss and replied also with equal formality. The gentlemen were expected to wear suits or jacket and trousers and even in the warmest weather ties were worn. The women were not allowed to wear trousers, even in the depths of winter. My colleague Bill Davis who was a Tax Officer (Higher Grade) anxiously enquired how my meeting had gone. A man of slightly less than middle height around forty-five years old with a great sense of humour he always took a great interest in my welfare. I therefore returned home feeling better but aware, with Mum and Dad right behind me I still had a mountain to climb . Mr Scattergood was a decent straightforward man in his middle fifties. Drawing on the inevitable cigarette he told me he would make arrangements for me to apply for the Civil Service exam. I with typical determination said that I also intended carrying on studying for my G C E's.

At this time my involvement with Spiritualism had been very little. I had read a few books on the subject and had often passed Charminster Road Spiritualist Church often promising myself one day I would take the courage to step inside. In my life I have come across so many coincidences, too numerous to mention. However I soon found out that Bill Davis's father had been a Medium before the War who had on many occasions worked at Charminster Road Spiritualist Church. Mr Dale was also convinced of Spiritualism and had received outstanding evidence from a well-known Bournemouth Medium Michael Aherne.

The Spiritualist Movement of the 1950's and 1960's still had quite a number of physical mediums producing various phenomena who travelled around the country demonstrating their gifts. So when Mr Dale heard that the well known medium William Olsen was visiting a small Spiritualist Church in Winton Bournemouth, The Silver Cross Psychic Research Centre, he booked three tickets for himself, Bill and Mr Scattergood. Afterwards Bill told me about the proceedings, the Séance took place in a small room in a very highly charged atmosphere that was increased by the singing of hymns before the session began. There must still be quite a few Spiritualists that remember sitting with Olsen and that Mrs Olsen's singing voice much to everyone's amusement was far from melodious. The Séance took place in a small room, attached to the church, about a dozen people being present. The Medium was first of all searched and then roped into his chair. Then further precautions were willingly made to eliminate all possibility of fraud. He had his jacket turned inside out and both buttoned and then sewn up. Olsen soon went into a deep trance breathing rather heavily, Mrs Olsen leading the singing in a robust way, everyone wondered what was going to happen next. A dim red bulb illuminated the room. Suddenly pandemonium broke out, two lightweight trumpets made of aluminium that had been standing in the centre of the room, rose from the floor, apparently unaided and started flying around at ceiling height very fast. The motion of the trumpets could be followed as they had been painted with luminous paint. Those present seated in a circle then experienced a skipping rope, situated in the centre of the circle being operated by unseen hands. Various voices claiming to be inhabitants of the Spiritual World including that of a little girl who claimed to be operating the skipping rope could be heard speaking through the trumpets. Throughout all this Olsen still in trance seemed to be totally unaware of what was going on. It was interesting to note that although the trumpets were flying around at breakneck speed seemingly by a miracle they did not hit anyone. At this stage Jack Scattergood felt an unseen dog on his lap moving around as though trying to get into a comfortable position. Needless to say there was no dog physically in the building at the time. As the séance was coming to an end they heard a loud bump, Olsen having seemingly been moved from one end of the room to another. What was more the jacket that had been sewn up was on the floor, Olsen was still tied up, apparently still in trance. The séance finally ended and the three taxmen were not sure what it all meant. However they were

21

thankful for the nearby Queen Victoria public house where they downed a few whiskies. There must be quite a few older Spiritualists who had similar experiences at William Olsen seances who would vouch for the dedication and honesty of this humble man

My interest in Spiritualism growing I now decided to attend a meeting at Charminster Road Spiritualist Church. Venturing into the unknown, a pleasant red bricked modern single storey building, I met a jolly, elderly man, short in stature who was handing out hymn books. Very smartly dressed with a carnation in his button-hole, although he had never met me before he greeted me like a long lost friend. I soon found myself comfortably seated in a wicker chair, I afterwards found out the church was well known for these chairs. Deciding to sit towards the back of the church {so that I could make a quick exit if need be} I was impressed by the warm and friendly atmosphere. Gradually the building filled up, mainly with middle aged or elderly people who seemed thankfully quite normal. Soon the row in front of me became quite full the seat directly in front of me being occupied by a lady with a large ornate hat. Finally two people took the platform the gentleman with the carnation who I discovered was the Chairman and a man I judged in his early sixties who was the Medium. The service began with a hymn sung with great enthusiasm by the sixty or so congregation. The carnation man then got up and introduced the medium. He in turn opened in prayer, which met with my approval. After another hymn sung to a familiar tune but words I did not know it was announced that the medium and his spirit inspirers would give the address.

The speaker wearing a smart grey suit spoke of his life before his conversion to Spiritualism as an army Padre in the African Sahara during the Second World War. He then spoke that death was not the end and given the right conditions those that died really could communicate with their loved ones left on Earth. I found myself enjoying this part of the meeting. Unlike some religious meetings the philosophy spoken seemed relevant to modern life and not distant and irrelevant. I found myself warming to this man and the cheerful people around me who like me seemed to take in every word. Finally after twenty-five minutes he sat down, a buzz of approval going around the church. The Chairman then announced another hymn after which there would be a demonstration of clairvoyance (whatever that was I wondered). This was as I was later to understand the standard format for most meetings. After the hymn an expectant hush filled the church there being the feeling the most important part was about to begin. The carnation man now announced " and now Mr McClega-han will link the two worlds for us all." I relaxed in my comfortable chair wondering what was going to happen next. The Medium pointed straight at me " I want to speak to that young man towards the back." I froze thinking he cannot mean me. I sank lower in my seat and was most thankful that the lady in front of me, with her large hat gave me cover. But the medium would not be denied and said " yes you behind the Lady with the hat." At this stage I looked up and down my row for salvation but alas there was no other young man but I. A kindly elderly Lady seated behind me whispered "he means you dear." It was too late to escape so I decided I had better

22

speak up. The Medium told me I was very mechanical and musically minded [both untrue]. He added that I had recently taken an examination and would pass it. Unusually enough for me I was confident of the outcome that I would pass. Three weeks later the results came.... I failed.

So my first experience of organised Spiritualism left me with mixed impressions. I liked the philosophy, format of the service and the obvious sincerity of all who took part. There had been no need to make a quick exit from the meeting after all. Although the message failed to impress me I was determined to investigate further.

I was now concentrating my efforts on improving my qualifications. Luckily Dad had heard of a lady teacher called Mrs Fredericks, who gave me private coaching in English. Though her fee of ten shillings a lesson put quite a hole in my weekly wage of seven pounds it turned out to be money very well spent as she was an excellent teacher and we got along well right from the beginning.

After some set backs under Mrs Fredericks gentle guidance I succeeded in passing three further GCE's and amazed myself by finishing twenty fifth in the national Civil Service Clerical Assistant examination after I had thought I had done hopelessly. Having studied Astronomy for a while I felt inspired to try to gain a GCE in this subject. Studying solely by myself I took the examination with two other students at Chelsea University. Only two of us completed the exam sharing the vast University Hall with people taking the Religious Knowledge exam. In due course I was re-warded with a pass so achieved finally, through dogged determination my target of five GCE's at ordinary level. Further progress was made passing the Civil Service Tax Officer exam and soon promotion to Tax Officer followed.

My investigations into Spiritualism continued, most weekends I attended the services at Charminster Road. Soon I was given the job of taking the collection plate around I suppose my first public work for the movement quite apt for a Taxman. Some of the mediums I saw particularly those from the Spiritualist Association Of Great Britain [SAGB] impressed me with their standard of platform work. In retrospect I did not realise how high the standard was. Many older Spiritualists will remember John Ambrose a cultured speaker always immaculately dressed with his neatly trimmed grey beard. Another well-known name Henry Richards a large Man with a big personality was also a frequent visitor. He became one of the founder members of The Institute Of Spiritualist Mediums. Less well known but equally impressive was May Jennings from New Malden, a retired school mistress, her work as a medium was in the same authoritarian manner. From the SAGB in London came such fine Mediums as Jack Mackay, Charles Horrey, Nan Whittle, Minie Bridges and Fred Jordan-Gill. Good local mediums included Cyril Curtis-Blake and Eve Hopkinson who in later years worked at the SAGB. Listening to all these wonderful Mediums gave me an excellent education and so many happy memories. Although at this time I had no wish to be a Medium seeing these people gave me in later years

23

when I started working the standard to which I should aspire. One day there was special excitement as Norah Blackwood, considered the best Medium in the country visited Charminster. I was lucky enough to witness her Clairvoyance that left everyone spellbound.

In a personal sense during this time I received few messages of real value. It seemed that many of the experienced Spiritualists received very evidential messages but I received much that was general and trivial. It was many years later that I worked out the reason for this. Many of the experienced Spiritualists had been receiving messages for many years. Consequently their loved ones in the Spiritual World were well used to this method of communication. My own contacts in the Spiritual World needed to get used to this procedure it is a thought worth consider-ing for new researchers. Some people when sitting with Mediums for the first time get outstanding results whilst others have to wait. The important thing to remember however, is the evidence is there, that it is obtainable for everyone as long as they investigate in a fair and honest way.

Whilst today more and more young people are being attracted to Spiritualism in the 1960's fewer youngsters were involved. Luckily it was inevitable that I would become friendly with other like-minded people of my age and I soon became a friend of Roger Rumble. He is the Grandson of the then senior trustee of Charmin-ster Road Church whose name was inscribed on the foundation stone of the Church when it was rebuilt around 1967. It was originally founded by Harry Hiscock, a local greengrocer and a brilliant healer, and Mrs Hayter a local clairvoyant of fine reputation. They devoted much time and energy to establish Spiritualism in the area. Two very fine portraits of these fine workers adorn the Church today. Another well known worker who graced the platform in the time leading up to my involvement was Horace Leaf FRGS who had travelled the World with Sir Arthur Conan Doyle that fine pioneer propagating Spiritualism. He was an engaging speaker and fine clairvoyant. Roger Rumble introduced me to Mrs Woodford a blind Bournemouth medium. She would be an outstanding influence in my psychic career.

I now decided to widen my spiritual search and pay a visit to Bath Road Spiritualist Church situated in the centre of Bournemouth. This well appointed Church is the longest established Spiritualist centre in the area, an early benefactor being Alfred Russell Wallace co-founder with Charles Darwin of " The Origin of Species." A past President of the Church had been Frank T Blake at one time President of the Spiritualist National Union, by all accounts a forceful and strong personality. My first impressions were that the Church was a little more formal than the centre at Charminster Road. The speaker and demonstrator was an elderly West Country Medium Clara Shakespeare still regarded by senior Spiritualists with great affection today. For some reason many Mediums served either one of the two major Churches in Bournemouth but not both. I was therefore introduced to many new workers including Winifred Franklyn who worked at The College Of Psychic Studies in London, Bertie Casaldini a character well known in Bournemouth who

24

was a retired Publican. For many years he was landlord of The Hare And Hounds in Springbourne so he had involvement professionally with both sorts of Spirits. Another very prominent worker was Grace Boyers the President who was the finest speaker I ever heard.

I now regularly attended services at Bath Road and saw many fine Mediums, new to me. Roy Morgan, Kathleen St George and Ursula Roberts impressed me greatly with the standard of of their philosophical talks as well as evidential Mediumship. The Medium who made the biggest impression was William Redmond, who I learned was senior Medium at S. A. G. B. Little did I realise that many years later I would become Senior Medium for the same organisation

The main problem with attending large public meetings is that one rarely gets an individual message so although many Mediums impressed me with their gifts and sincerity I was still seeking that individual proof of survival that seemed as elusive as ever.

At this time my social life was extending further and I was obtaining new friends and acquaintances although I still kept in contact with several old school friends and belonged to several Youth Clubs where I particularly enjoyed playing Table Tennis. Pop music was becoming all the rage and a band called The Beatles from Liverpool were becoming popular I was never a fan. The more rebellious teenagers followed the Rolling Stones. We started going to various dances around the Town; a very young Tony Blackburn would play the guitar during the interval at The Pavilion. A young group called Manfred Mann were starting to make a name for themselves at a resident gig at the Disc A Go Go at the Lansdowne. I also remember Zoot Money was about in Bournemouth at this time. One day at Youth Club we were all seated in this room having a discussion when I saw a number of coloured lights around a girl called Bella who in truth I did not like. At first I naturally thought it was a trick of the light but after several experiments including moving my position rejected this theory. I was very puzzled by this and whilst I was pondering this all of a sudden Bella flew out the room slamming the door in a rage. I later discovered that I had seen her aura made easier by her highly emotional state. Since then I have seen many thousands of auras and have resulted in a lifetime's study of this fascinating subject.

I started my investigation into Spiritual Healing and attended a large Spiritual Healing demonstration taken by the world renowned Healer Harry Edwards. Naturally deciding to obtain healing for my poor vision two well-respected local healers Bill Uren and Ron Reeves were recommended to me. From the beginning they promised nothing but I was hugely impressed by their dedication. One day seated in the healing waiting room at the top of the stairs I was joined by a lady who had the appointment after mine. We started talking and she told me that three weeks previously she had to be carried up the stairs, her mobility had become so very limited the

Doctors had given up on her. Being told no treatment was available she resigned herself to severely restricted mobility for the rest of her life. However someone told her about spiritual healing she previously having no experience of the subject she had decided she had nothing to lose. Now just three weeks later she could walk up the stairs unaided. . Bill was also a superb trance medium whose guide was Doctor Scott an Ophthalmic Surgeon who lived in Blackburn in the early 1900's. No charge was ever made for healing a collection plate being situated in an obscure corner of the sanctuary for those wanting to make a voluntary donation. I wish I had got to know these two superb gentlemen better.

In Spiritualism more young people were becoming interested. At the SAGB two young mediums Robin Stevens and David Young were causing a big impression particularly with their willingness to experiment with their gifts. Soon in London owing to popular demand an organisation connected and sympathetic to the ideals of Spiritualism but operated by young people was started and named The Psychic Youth Group. Soon similar organisations were formed in the provinces and when a group was formed in Bournemouth I became very involved. We formed a committee arranged to hire a hall for our first public meeting and then set everything up to organise publicity for our group. For weeks we distributed hundreds of leaflets standing in the town centre handing out the information and talking to interested passers-by. We wondered whether we would cover our costs but need not have worried, {perhaps we were guided from the beyond} for our first meeting saw a good turnout. Two Mediums gave a demonstration of clairvoyance, one of whom Chris Batchelor, then a young man living in Southampton went on to devote many years to the movement in particular being involved with Kilmarnock Church in Scotland. Although subsequent Psychic Youth Group meetings were less well attended we attracted a hard core of about thirty members that supported our activities. It was good to mix with and become friendly with people of a like mind and soon the group became a thriving social scene, connections being made with neighbouring groups particularly with Southampton and Salisbury. Naturally quite a few romances developed and in due course a number of marriages took place between members who had met at Psychic Youth Group meetings. Although I was still shy the implications of the possibility of a romance for me within the group was not lost on me. When a decision was made to form a Circle to develop members' psychic abilities I decided to join. Not I may add for any great desire to become a Medium but because the object of my affections was also joining the Circle. Soon after starting to sit my psychic abilities started to manifest but my romantic life also took a step forward when I started to date the girl I had my eye on. Truly falling in love especially for the first time is a magical experience.

The Committee at Charminster Road Church as helpful as ever gave us use of the church, so we held our developing group on a Thursday night when no other activity

26

was taking place. One of the most difficult things in psychic development is to prove to yourself that your visualisation is not imagination. Confirmation of this happened one night in a most unexpected way. This particular evening Roger Rumble and myself arrived early for our session. Within a few minutes from our position seated inside we both heard clearly footsteps of someone walking up to the front door of the Church. We then both saw a figure through the opaque glass on the door separating the corridor from the area inside the church. This figure appeared to walk pass the door into the hall at the back of the building. We both naturally thought the figure was a member of the church who seeing the building open incorrectly thought it was open for a public meeting. Not thinking in any way the appearance was of a psychic nature in fact this was the last thing on our minds we both immediately got up to inform our visitor that it was a private session, attendance of which was by invitation only. Imagine our surprise therefore on reaching the corridor that there was no sight of our visitor. Since it was a virtual impossibility for the person to have left the building without our knowledge we were puzzled that a thorough search revealed we were the only occupants. We were left trying to find a logical explanation to all this. I may add for the record that the exit door was under observation throughout. The value of this experience was not so much what was seen or heard that was relatively unremarkable . It was that both of us had the same impressions without at first thinking it was anything else but a normal physical happening. Our immediate collaboration gave strength and credence to the experience. The incident made us come to the conclusion that the visitor was from the Spiritual World. It confirmed to both of us that in our psychic development we were receiving an increase in our awareness of things of this nature.

In 1968 due to my promotion to Tax Officer I spent quite a lot of time in London on training courses. The training centre was at Honeypot Lane Canons Park, the buildings being prefabricated structures that apparently housed Italian Prisoners of war during World War Two. I do not know what the Italians thought of it but I found the accommodation boiling hot in summer and freezing cold in winter. Luckily the local " Green Man." public house provided a more relaxed and comfortable location. During my time on training courses I found lodgings with Mrs Rogers a kind elderly lady who paid special attention to her house guests. I soon found out from my fellow trainees that I was lucky in my choice. Mr Rogers a short stocky man worked on The London Underground as a Booking Clerk and had spent his early years in the RAF. In his service days he had been friendly with Douglas Bader the famous air ace who continued to fly despite the handicap of losing both his legs. As I so enjoyed staying with Mr and Mrs Rogers during the next few years I resided with them for holidays as well as for training courses. This gave me plenty of opportunity to pay many visits to The Spiritualist Association Of Great Britain [SAGB] in Belgrave Square London to continue my investigations.

Travelling on the Underground to Hyde Park Corner I wondered what adventures of a spiritual nature awaited me at the SAGB. My journey was soon completed as I

27

walked the short distance between the Tube Station and the Associations headquarters just a short distance from Buckingham Palace. As I entered the building I was pleasantly surprised at the large number of younger people of my age group around. I soon learned that the building is of special historical and architectural interest and is situated in one of the finest Squares in London. As I booked my group sitting with a Medium named Jack Mackay I took in the busy atmosphere and glanced up at the magnificent staircase sweeping up from the Reception Hall to the floors above. I soon found myself in a small room in the Dowding Wing named after Air Chief Marshall Lord Dowding, hero of The Battle of Britain who was a convinced Spiritualist. Both he and Lady Dowding worked for many years propagating the truths of Spiritualism. As I waited with expectation for the sitting to begin I was struck at how different the five of us all strangers gathered for this session. Spiritualism I thought must have a wide appeal to all sections of the community. Finally Jack Mackay arrived, a short slender man in his late 70's I judged. The Medium speaking with a strong Scottish accent began the session. I waited patiently whilst after a prayer he addressed each person in turn in a direct forthright manner. From their answers my fellow sitters seemed to know what he was talking about. Finally he turned to me, " you work for the Crown, the Civil Service and you have recently been promoted". I acknowledged this information to be correct. Mackay went on to say " Your Grandmother is here, your Mother's Mother [there followed a brief but accurate character analysis of both Grandmother and me.] She is guiding you and there is much spiritual work for you to do." After the session I analysed the results. .I had certainly obtained a good insight into both my character and present circumstances. I definitely felt it was worth going back for more. On subsequent visits to the SAGB I had various sittings with such fine mediums as Roy Morgan, Magdalene Kelly, Ronald Kelly and Freda Fell messages of a similar nature and theme being given. Nearly always the same grandmother communicated. The results were interesting but did not totally convince. In truth I had not received totally convincing proof of survival. The obvious integrity and honesty of the Mediums had however struck me. There were no attempts to fish for information.I was not asked for any details but told facts. I had certainly the impression through these sessions that I was also getting to know myself better. Also impressive and these feelings have stayed with me all these years and is common to so many Spiritualists I have met was the cordiality, friendliness and sincerity of all those involved in the subject. I was therefore determined to investigate Spiritualism further.

Away from the spiritual scene my social life continued to expand. In London on the training courses in the evenings we had great times. One night a whole group of us decided to have a night out and we ended up, about a dozen of us in a sleazy Strip Club in Soho my one and only visit to such an establishment. I cannot say the experience was in the slightest way erotic. The climax of the show was when one of the not so young lady performers sneezed and because she had so few items of clothes on she wiped her nose with her arm. Obviously we all exploded in laughter and since our behaviour was upsetting some of the regular patrons we wisely decided to leave the club rather quickly.

My times attending meetings at the SAGB were thoroughly enjoyed. I attended many public demonstrations some were held in "The Conan Doyle Hall" named after the author of "The Sherlock Holmes Stories" which contains the original chair used by Sir Arthur at the time he wrote these books. Others took place in "The Oliver Lodge Hall " named after the famous scientist who became a convinced Spiritualist . It contains a valuable Adams fireplace. At these meetings I would get a feel for the medium whether or not I felt on their vibration. The most impressive medium at these public demonstrations was Norah Blackwood. In her demonstrations when the communication was flowing she frequently gave fact after fact. Full names, addresses, dates of birth; the most intimate details of both the communicators and recipient's life. Such was the standard of her work that she was invited to demonstrate at The SAGB Annual Service of Reunion at the Royal Albert Hall a record eight times. Obviously with such outstanding ability she was booked up for sittings months ahead. In the end I managed to sit with her in private and group sittings on four occasions but got nothing of real value. Perhaps she was just not on my vibration. Over the years I have seen and heard many mediums however none come anyway near to Norah Blackwood in her ability to consistently produce outstanding evidence. It is a pity that there are relatively few people around now who saw her as I feel her mediumship should be used as a yardstick to others. Certainly no public Medium working today comes anywhere near to her standard.

My own psychic development had already started with the Psychic Youth Group circle. I had been invited to Mrs Woodford's group several times as a guest. The fellow circle members were the usual mixtures of sincere and dedicated Spiritualists trying to develop their psychic potential in the sympathetic atmosphere. Regretfully some have overactive imaginations. One week a rather intense lady said, " I see Ducks" everyone seemed to ignore her comment. The next week she saw pies, to which I remarked to everyone else's amusement "those were the ducks you saw last week." When in a subsequent week she saw "a red crocodile " again those present took little notice. The following week when we gathered we knew the reason why, the famous horse race The Grand National had been run on the intervening Saturday and a horse named Red Alligator had just won. Mrs Woodford was a highly respected Medium. Although she had been totally blind for a number of years she still had an independent life style. She obviously saw in me certain potential so when I was offered a permanent place in her home group I immediately accepted. Under her gentle guidance my Spiritual gifts started to develop and within a few weeks of sitting all the intuitive feelings I had as a child came back. In those days you would not have dreamed of starting your public work until your circle leader told you the correct time you ready. Mrs Woodford was very much "old school" and that a slow sure development was always far better than a quick sensational one.

One of the leading lights of the local Spiritualist movement was Eric Lamb, who had been a fighter pilot in World War Two. He was a Minister Of The Spiritualist National Union [MSNU] which is the highest award that is offered by that organisation. Together with his wife Bessie they for many years were the mainstays of Christchurch Spiritualist Church. It was Eric who gave me my first opportunity in 1969 to make my platform debut at Christchurch. Once Mrs Woodford had confirmed I was ready for such a big step I nervously took my first public speaking engagement. Sharing the meeting with Eric was a wonderful experience his demonstrations of clairvoyance were always good. In later years he always supported me in my Spiritual work.

There are many different forms of mediumship some to the newcomer seem too sensational to be true. Transfiguration is when the Spiritual guides are able to build over a mediums face facsimile features of someone passed over who often is then able through the medium who is usually in trance to give a personal message. It may sound far-fetched but if the Bible is to be believed [Matthew xv ii] this can happen. At this time many forms of mediumship were becoming rarer so when a Transfiguration medium came to Charminster Road Church several of us Psychic Youth Group members got front row seats for the meeting. The room was in almost total darkness, the only light coming from a red lamp placed near to the Mediums face. He showed on his facial features a considerable experience of life the dramatic effect being enhanced with a patch over one eye. During the séance although one or two claimed to be able to see a change of features, the hall being packed to capacity, neither I nor the vast majority of people present saw anything. Around this time another Transfiguration medium Queenie Nixon was producing convincing phenomena. It is to my everlasting regret that I did not see her work.

Apart from the two main Spiritualist churches there were various smaller organisations in Bournemouth. One was The Silver Crosse Psychic Research Centre in Winton run by Bessie Crosse who was not easy to get along with at the best of times. Mrs Crosse could be very blunt in her remarks and only a few workers had the tolerance to serve her for long. One day attending her church I was introduced to Lewis Wood a sincere and dedicated local Medium, who was placid enough to serve her church regularly. Mrs Crosse said, " this is Lewis Wood he purports to be a Medium." Lewis offered his hand in a firm handshake and greeted me with a friendly "Brummie" accent not the slightest way perturbed by her comments and carried on as though nothing had happened.

In many ways the Medium that transformed my life was Fred Jordan- Gill originally from Devon he served the SAGB for thirty-seven years and became its senior Medium. I listened with fascination not only to his high standard of mediumship but also to his talks. His story of how he originally came into Spiritualism is typical of many. As a youngster he was aware he was different from other people but could not understand why. One day he was walking through Exeter on his way to hospital when he saw a notice " If you want to know where the dead are step in" so he stepped in. Inside was an old Devonshire lady Mrs Ada Tower who told him that he would have an operation on the arm and have a bone taken out. In due course there was a lot of concern and talk of his arm being amputated. He then witnessed a Spiritual vision that gave him much peace and optimism. He received healing and after a simple operation when a bone was removed he had no more problems.

Luckily Jordan-Gill was resident in Bournemouth so he was a frequent worker at both the major churches there. Speaking with a strong West Country accent in his public demonstrations he had a strong forthright manner, moving his delicate hands in elegant gestures. Immediately I liked and respected him and I reached a crossroads in my life. Would I dedicate my time to the Spiritualist movement or would I leave Spiritualism and devote my ideals to my growing political philosophy? My fascination with politics was due to my idealism; some would say naivety that the individual can make a difference. I decided in May 1970 to have a private sitting with him to see what transpired. This sitting was a turning point, he looked at me with his piercing blue eyes for a moment, and then he described with accuracy the position I was in. There followed a perfect description of Grandmother {as usual Mum's side} a good character picture of her and certain intimate information only she could have known. Then followed certain highly relevant points appertaining to my personal life. These were gone into in great depth, the statements given completely true. The sitting so impressed me that I persuaded Mum and Dad to also sit with Jordan-Gill who obviously did not know them. Mum in particular obtained fascinating results and became convinced of the psychic faculty. In later years I became quite friendly with him and he told me many fascinating things about his research into the truths of Spiritualism. His father had passed over when Fred was only two months old. At a Direct Voice séance [I will describe the phenomena of Direct Voice later in the book} his Father spoke to him gave his Mothers maiden name and said he had Fred's brother with him. Jordan-Gill always understood he was an only child but his Father insisted a six and a half-month boy had been born. On going home his Mother confirmed everything was true only her and his Father had known these facts. In later years I had the pleasure of taking and sharing meetings with him and he always encouraged me in my work. One day on meeting Mum and Dad he told them should I wish to go forward with my psychic development I would do very well. Truly he transformed my life and largely through his influence I now decided to devote even more time to Spiritualism.

My romantic life was moving forward and four of us decided to go on holiday together to The Spiritualist National Union Summer School held in Penarth in South Wales. Obviously the combination of the Spiritual and the romantic appealed to me as it did with the other members of our party. In fact my friends Geoff and Karen decided at the end of the holiday they would like to get married and so they did. . During our time at the Summer School we met many interesting characters including Mr Verity then well into his nineties who talked a lot about the pioneers of Spiritualism. We also met the future President of the Spiritualist National Union Eric Hatton, Percy Wilson a past President of the SNU a man of very wide experience and Robin

31

Stevens then an up and coming young Medium. His work was excellent but he was aggressive and difficult to get along with. Sally Ferguson an elderly lady from the Midlands also impressed me with her sincerity and no nonsense approach to her clairvoyance.

The highlight to the activities was a materialisation experiment with Gordon Higginson. The audience was a very large one and as the ideal number for such a meeting was twenty the one hundred and forty gathered was considered far too large. It was understood that not since the 1860's had a physical medium operated under such conditions. The Medium was seated in a wooden cabinet with a dark green curtain on the front with a string drawcord. There were no secret compartments in the cabinet and no trap doors on the stage where the cabinet was situated. As usual I managed to get a front row seat. Higginson wearing a dark shirt soon became entranced. Invisible hands rolled up the curtain seemingly and a vapour like substance was clearly seen coming from the Medium's mouth. This substance for a while lay on his chest and then expanded until it reached the floor. Then suddenly it drifted upwards until it was the shape and height of a man. Throughout this the atmosphere in the hall was electric. Yet I had an inner feeling of peace to me what I was seeing was genuine and good. It was frustrating that you could not see the individual features of the form. However the form spoke in a strong Midlands accent "Sally Sally its me Bert". With that Sally Ferguson the medium spoke and the two {Bert was her Husband who had passed over} had an intimate conversation both recalling personal incidents. After a short time the form disintegrated and the séance ended truly a memorable experience for all present.

It seemed at this time after the frustration of not getting totally convincing evidence that the Spiritual World were totally determined to prove their presence to me. I continued sittings at the SAGB, and arranged a session with Charles Horrey who had greatly impressed me at public demonstrations. As I entered the room in "The Lord Dowding Wing" Charles, a fairly tall sensitive looking man in his early fifties looked drained and tired. Perhaps lacking diplomacy I mentioned this fact to him. His reply was to the effect it had been a long day and every sitter had been difficult so he was not really in the mood to give me a sitting but he would try, however three no's would mean the sitting would be terminated. Charles then closed his eyes and within a few minutes started speaking. " Your Grandmother is here, her name was Winifred, she sends much love to your Mum and Dad." Horrey went on to describe changes in my work, that I had recently transferred to a different section. He then went on to say that the change would be advantageous to me this turned out to be completely correct. Other accurate details followed, including the comment that Grandma liked Mum and Dad's new bungalow. This was highly significant and relevant statement as my parents had managed to buy this property their first with money left by Grandmother. I left the session very impressed walking on air. The evidence had been superb. Some months later I decided to sit with Charles Horrey again. I made sure I booked his first session of the day. In he came into the room bright and cheerful full of the joys of spring looking happy and relaxed. It was a warm pleasant day when one should feel good about the World. He sat down, could get nothing for me and said " friend I am not the Medium for you please go back to reception to get your money back." I had a tremendous respect for his honesty. Charles Horrey was a brilliant Medium. Regretfully I feel he did not, in his lifetime gain the recognition his work deserved. I am pleased that Betty Shine in her books pays tribute to him for setting her on her spiritual road.

Coral Polge was the most outstanding Psychic artist of her generation and rightly became a legend in her own lifetime. In later years I would share the platform with her many times but all this was well in the future. I had managed to obtain a private sitting with her. She drew an elderly man making the comment he was my great Grandfather on Mother's side of the family and his name was Henry. I told Coral I would have to check this information as I had little knowledge of his life still, less of his appearance. I arrived home and put the portrait on the kitchen table. Mum immediately said " that is a picture of Granddad how did you get it"? She also confirmed his name was Henry. Such evidence certainly gave the whole family food for thought. Within a relatively short length of time I had received excellent evidence of survival through several forms of mediumship by different Mediums The Spiritual World were certainly making their presence felt.

Away from Spiritualism a General Election took place, the Labour party was expected to win with a comfortable majority but for once the opinion polls got it all wrong. The Liberal party under the leadership of the gifted Jeremy Thorpe faced an uphill battle. As always I stayed up to watch the results. As always the television cameras were "live" at the declaration for the party leaders. The candidates for the constituency of North Devon lined up as the Returning Officer made his declaration. It was a grim faced but relieved Jeremy Thorpe that was the victor but only with a wafer thin majority of three hundred and sixty nine. The election was a disaster for the Liberal party their number of MPs being reduced to six, three of whom John Pardoe in Cornwall David Steel in Scotland and Jeremy Thorpe hung on with majorities of under one thousand. They were left with only three safe seats Russell Johnson and Jo Grimond in Scotland and Emlyn Hooson in Wales. The Conservatives swept to an unlikely victory.

My romantic life took a turn for the worse for on 5th November 1970 my first true love finished our relationship. It did not come as a shock as things had not been good for sometime, however I am sure everyone that has the experience of this happening, that part of our illusions about life disappear forever. Of course life sometimes is tough, somehow however we have to find the resilience to go on when it is easier to give up. Such incidents weaken our confidence yet from inside we gain strength. People interested in developing their Spiritual gifts sometimes do not appreciate the downside. In attempting to develop this sensitivity one forgets we are making ourselves more sensitive to outside things and everyday events that perhaps other people are not so sensitive to.

The development of the psychic gift should of course be taken very seriously; some people only play at the subject. The student should have knowledge of not only the various psychic centres but the likely results of deliberately opening up these chakras or centres. In fact Spiritualist leaders need to educate not only those entering the movement but some already in it, of the dangers this can involve. This is no idle threat for example ignorance of the use of the Kundalini can result in big problems. Let me explain the Kundalini is the Spiritual energy connected with the opening of the chakra centres. Particularly the Eastern mystical schools recognise the connection between sexual energy and the energy required for psychic and spiritual activity. This is why many Yoga's and spiritual teachers in the East practice celibacy. Although those in the east are certainly able from a more knowledgeable background to do this I am not unsympathetic to this viewpoint. However one has to be most careful in this area. The dealing with these energies either way, need the strictest discipline. I know of one or two psychics that lost control in this area with disastrous consequences. Certainly I advocate moderation in all things when dealing with the finely attuned energies required for this sort of work.

I do not regret my pathway though the pain of sometimes feeling apart and different at a time when I so wanted to belong had an effect upon me. Not being physically strong and the memories of being bullied have given me a greater understanding for those in similar circumstances. I hope that it has made me a more compassionate man. I felt terribly left out and left behind when my friends started learning to drive and acquiring cars. I knew because of my poor vision it would be something I would never be able to do. Those with similar restrictions will be able to fully understand and appreciate my feelings. All this has made me go into the depths of my psyche or inner self. Sometimes people say to me that it must be marvellous to be a Medium to have this Spiritual vision. But often they do not realise the price to be paid in increased sensitivity. However if we have a gift for helping others, do we ignore that gift and run away from our Spiritual responsibilities. Or do we face up to it control it as much as possible and in helping others we help ourselves. This was the dilemma facing me at this time . So I decided to make every effort to move forward in my life and became even more determined to develop and use my latent talents.

At this time I spent quite a lot of time socialising with my friends in the centre of town. The Royal Exeter Hotel became almost a second home; a building with a fascinating history including it is rumoured a resident ghost although I have never seen it. It was the first house to be built in Bournemouth, which is essentially a modern town that only really started to grow in Victorian times. One day I bought an imitation leather coat and walked proudly into the Royal Exeter. George, the Austral-ian barman said " I like your plastic coat." I accepted the joke with good humour but was determined to get my own back. The opportunity soon came; George made the error of telling me he had never seen snow. Due to my instigation I was well known and had a lot of acquaintances people entering the bar asked him " seen snow yet George?" After a few weeks of a dozen or so customers a night asking him the same

34

question the joke wore off. Some time later I was out with the lads in the Royal Exeter when this stranger came up and in no uncertain terms told me that a newly married man should not be out on the town. Obviously being single at the time I queried this observation only to be given a photograph supplied by George the barman showing a guy strongly resembling me in his wedding picture. The stranger took some convincing it was not a picture of me. There was an interesting sequel to this; some weeks later I went into a gentleman's outfitters to be subject to a serious case of mistaken identity. Again it took a lot of explaining to confirm who I was. They say everybody has a double it is a pity I never, at least to date, got to know mine.

In 1973 Mrs Woodford informed me, much to my amazement, that she considered I was ready for the public platform as a Medium. So I started gradually taking one or two services with her at New Milton and other small venues around the Bournemouth area. After each meeting at Circle the next week we would critically go through my work together. Then after a while she let me go out on my own to take meetings but always either attending herself or sending someone to analyse the standard of my work. It was a tough but good training for me. Not only was my mediumistic work and capabilities as a speaker constructively commented upon but also my standard and style of my appearance and the way I generally conducted myself. Gradually I was invited to more places in the Bournemouth area, Poole, Parkstone, Kinson, Christchurch great training ground for my newly developing gifts.

I was invited to Charminster that was so special to me as I had spent so many happy hours listening to so many fine Mediums there . In those days new Mediums were usually tried out on the Thursday evening service and if found suitable invited to take the week-end services. It seems that I must have done fairly well as I was invited back to take other services. In fact it is a source of pride that I have served this Spiritual centre on a regular basis and like a considerable number of other churches and societies its longest serving Medium. Committees operate all Spiritualist churches and at each committee meeting the work of each Medium is discussed carefully. Particularly at the larger organisations a high standard of mediumship is required.

Every church has a few members whom for one reason or another claim every message that is not immediately placed. One day a church official was talking to a man who regularly tried to claim any message. He said, "You know you are very gullible at times. If I gave you a camel from the spiritual world you would accept it". The gentleman replied " too right I would I was in the Camel Corps in the War." There are people in the local spiritualist movement that I have known for years. Yet I know little or nothing of their personal lives. Take Wyn Clarke President of Charminster Road for a long time. She has chaired for me on countless occasions yet I know next to nothing about her family . One day taking a meeting with her I turned around as we were sharing the platform: -

35

Hayward: - " Your Mother is here and talking about Tina".

Mrs Clarke: - " That is my daughter".

Hayward: - " Your Mother tells me you should expect a happy event".

Mrs Clarke: - {laughing} " I know nothing about that".

A few days later I got an exciting telephone call from Wyn " Remember that message you gave me last week well Tina's expecting". We still remind each other of this all these years later.

On another occasion whilst demonstrating at another local centre I saw clairvoyantly a well-known member of the congregation named Miss Thorpe. I thought she was still alive and so did the other members. The communicating spirit said otherwise. A few days later the church officials received confirmation of her passing the previous week.

Having been closely involved with the Spiritualist movement for so many years people often ask me if the standard of mediumship has fallen. The plain answer is yes without a doubt. I admit that today there are still many fine Mediums a considerable number of which work behind the scenes away from the limelight. However social conditions have changed and many now simply do not have the patience to sit for development for years and years without guarantee of results.

Today instead of working within the organisations already in place many open new centres of there own. Whilst I accept that the motivation of some are very sincere, others are operated by " inflated egos" whose motivation is questionable. Some of the smaller organisations are well run, offer a good standard of facilities, very reasonable quality of mediumship and are a credit to Spiritualism. Indeed some were very helpful and supportive in my early career. However the truth in my view, is that there is much failing in the training of Mediums and because there are too many churches and societies too many potential Mediums are encouraged to start public work far too early. I was taught to wait until my teacher told me I was ready. There is the world of difference between giving accurate clairvoyance in the co-cooned atmosphere of a sympathetic circle quite another in the more demanding atmosphere of a public meeting.

My other interests outside Spiritualism continued although even then I found my psychic faculties useful. Although society was less violent than today you still had to keep your wits about you. On more than one occasion on my insistence we left certain pubs or clubs just before a fracas took place. At one time if quick action had not been taken I may well of ended up in Poole Quay. Being unable to swim it would have been a desperate situation. Many times we ended up in the comparative calm of the Royal Exeter. Another favourite venue was the Royal Ballrooms in Boscombe.

Right from the beginning I made a pact with the spiritual guides that assist me that unless it was a desperately urgent situation I would not wish to have spiritual vision in a non-working environment. This is something that I have always believed in very strongly, to be master of my mediumship rather than my mediumship become

36

master of me. Like every other profession some Mediums never switch off, I do not consider that to be a good thing. However the one area of my work where this does not apply is the seeing of auras something I have always found fascinating. So often around the clubs and bars of Bournemouth, I would study with fascination the auras of various individuals. Although I never hid from my friends that I used my psychic gifts professionally they found it difficult to understand why I was attracted to certain people whilst others I stayed completely clear of.

For the first time since the famous F A Cup run of 1957 Bournemouth Football Club were starting to go places. In the 1969/70 season they had been relegated to the fourth division for the first time in their history. Obviously drastic measures had to be made and Harold Walker the ambitious chairman of the club appointed a new young manager John Bond. Soon promotion was achieved with the help of prolific goalscorer Ted Macdougal who in an F A Cup game that I attended with Dad once scored nine goals. I was one of many supporters who travelled up to Birmingham where a record crowd of 48000 saw Bournemouth lose a crucial third division promotion match 2-1 to Aston Villa. Regretfully Bournemouth faltered following the pattern of previous years and was pipped for promotion by Aston Villa. For several seasons the club very nearly got promotion for the first time in their history to the second division but alas it was not to be until many years in the future. Nevertheless it was exciting times supporting our local team.

It was also exciting times supporting Hampshire Cricket Club who in 1973 won the County Championship rather unexpectedly. The batting was especially strong with one of the best opening partnerships in the World with Barry Richards and Gordon Greenidge. Actually some years later I dated, for a short while, a young lady who had gone out with Barry Richards when they both lived in South Africa. Quite a come down for her going from world class sportsman to me.

I was now becoming quite well known on the local circuit as a reliable speaker and demonstrator. Right from the start I had been determined to try and give accurate and honest information. Too many Mediums try to tell people information they want to hear rather than what they get. So it is important not to expand or edit what is given. The main purpose of psychic work is to transfer information in an open way, avoiding vague statements that are confusing, leaving the recipient to accept or reject what is offered. I also commenced giving private consultations. I have always enjoyed the one to one aspects in a private session perhaps more than public meetings. I was learning, as every Medium must do to trust what is given from spirit. It is essential to get into close rapport with ones individual guides. Even in these early days I was intrigued by the ingenuity of the spiritual world. On one occasion I obtained the name of the village in India my sitters originated from.

The question of guides within the Spiritualist movement is an interesting one. In my early investigations into spiritual matters various Mediums described various guides to me. To my sceptical mind the multitudes of Red Indians, Chinese, Zulu's, given to me seemed too sensational to be true. They reminded me of characters from a Christmas pantomime and obviously thought they were products of someone's fertile imagination. Of course many people outside of the Spiritualist movement accept they have a Guardian Angel watching over them. The Spiritualists soon explained to me that each of us have several guides those from the spiritual world who wish to inspire us forward. They are often from the so-called primitive races that live nearer to nature. Because of this they are apparently ideally suited for understanding the true spiritual purpose of life. Still my logical mind found it difficult to accept this I reasoned that this may be acceptable in theory but in practice Mediums described these individuals when they had a "dry" period. After all one could neither prove or disprove the existence of these people. So far so good but then various Mediums started to describe this Chinese guide with matching description time and time again. Still my critical and sceptical mind would not accept what I was being constantly given. Finally we reached a stage that the same name was given of this guide by several Mediums of good repute. So slowly very slowly I managed using my own psychic vision to build a picture of this man. I suppose what finally convinced me of his reality was a portrait of him drawn by a psychic artist that matched totally all the information acquired over a considerable period of time. What is more even the name checked out. I freely accept this in an area of Spiritualism that can be open to wishful thinking. I am certainly not an advocate of guide worship. Some Mediums say my guide says this and my guide says that. I think this is unhealthy as I consider it is wrong to worship Guides and isn't the way forward. I cannot even claim with my perception that my guide is someone who I am constantly aware of. However I do know he is often in the background helping and guiding in his individual quiet way.

My growing reputation as a Medium now took me outside of the immediate Bournemouth area. Particular pleasure was taken at serving Southampton [Cavendish Grove] church. The President was Elsie Crespin truly one of the spiritual and loving souls I have ever met. A fine Medium herself she was a wonderful ambassador for Spiritualism everyone who came into her presence felt how special she was. I am forever grateful for her help and guidance in those early years. Her friend Nellie Milne who had been involved with the movement for so many years is also worth special mention for her kindness and support. Indeed although in Spiritualism I have met certain people who I have not got along with the vast majority of Spiritualists are kindness itself. "Pop" and Mrs Aldridge who ran the church until well into there nineties operated another Spiritual centre I served from the lounge of a detached house in Parkstone. Cecil Dyer a Minister of the Spiritualist National Union was President of Parkstone SNU Church for more than forty years. A small neat man always smart in appearance he engaged my friend Geoff Griffiths and I to share a service Geoff an engaging speaker giving the address whilst I demonstrated clairvoyance a combination that was successful and repeated on quite a number of occasions. In fact it is a pity in Spiritualism we do not have more combinations of this nature . It is asking a lot to expect a first class address to be followed by a brilliant demonstration. The vibrations needed for both these activities are so totally different.

My interest in politics continued and during the period between the General Elections of 1970 and 1974 the Liberal party achieved, much to my delight, a fair amount of success at by elections. In 1972 Rochdale was gained by Cyril Smith a larger than life character if ever there was one. There were also spectacular gains at Sutton and Cheam and in July 1973, Isle of Ely {by Clement Freud} and Ripon. This was followed by a narrow victory at Berwick where Alan Beith unseated the Conservative. I have always believed politics and religion perhaps the two subjects that cause most conflicts and derision to be a personal affair. I do not seek to convert or convince anyone that my pathway is right for other people. My truth is my truth and your truth is your truth. We all form our own opinions from our own experiences. But neither do I shy away from friendly debate and discussion. Whilst I nail my colours to the mast I totally respect any other democratic view. Although I may not agree with the views of others I defend to the death their right to express it. Especially as a Spiritualist still a misunderstood minority I do expect reciprocal action back. The problem with so many opponents of Spiritualism is quite frankly they make pronouncements very often from a position of ignorance.

Annie James the Medium's secretary at Bath Road Church was of the old school. She telephoned me to invite me to serve the church. She made it clear she was extremely selective whom she had on her platform and that I should consider it an honour so early in my career to serve Bath Road. It was obviously a sign I had arrived. A lot of local Mediums of good repute and many years standing had not in those days been given this opportunity. In fact even Mrs Woodford who was a very fine Medium had not been given the chance to work there. So the day arrived when I nervously took the platform under the watchful eye of May Watts the elegant refined President it was rumoured the more decorative the hat she wore the more she approved of the Medium. Mrs Woodford was there as always to give support and constructive comments afterwards. Anyway everyone seemed to approve and again I now have the pleasure of looking back at serving this centre for nearly thirty continuous years.

One of my early public demonstrations at Bath Road Church resulted in lasting consequences that I could not have foreseen at the time. Giving messages to a group sat together I indicated that as they were so much in tune with each other they should form a developing group. May I point out that the one ingredient for a successful Spiritual circle is harmony, this is essential for good results. After the meeting I was approached by the group who agreed with the messages I had given them. They were thinking of forming a developing group as I had suggested. They then asked if I could be the circle leader a request I was pleased to accept. The resulting home circle has operated with various changes of personnel for well over a quarter of a century. Two members have been with me all that time and we have had interesting results over the years with various gifts of the spirit. Predominantly it is a circle where the clairvoyant gifts are developed and used. As with every other worthwhile group different members bring in different attributes. Some create much power whilst others are developing their individual gifts at their own pace. Over the years much evidence has

39

been given some of a strictly personal nature . One interesting message stands out, I informed one member her front passenger tyre was faulty. She was most surprised, as she had recently had new tyres fitted. However as she was planning a long journey she decided to get the matter checked out. Her regular mechanic checked the car tyres thoroughly and could find nothing wrong. She then requested that he should double check and told him that a Medium had told her it was faulty. With some amusement the mechanic rechecked the position and found a fault in the front passenger tyre that was not obvious on his first inspection. In fact the fault could have had very serious consequences if travelling at high speed. Since much of her impending journey was to be by motorway the importance of the message was obvious. Down the years in our private group a very high standard of evidence has been produced by a considerable number of members. Also many guests have attended by invitation as our group's private nature is in my opinion one of its greatest assets and received fine evidence. So in our own small way we have been spreading spiritual truths for a long time. The beautiful harmony of our meetings is certainly beneficial to all. At the time of writing two members have developed their mental gifts to a professional standard, although at present for various reasons they do not wish to work in the public arena.

My social life continued and with my friends I had many adventures. My main friends were Max (the musician), Roy (the beard), Ken (the farmer) and Jim (the footballer) all characters. There were several on the edge of our group including Keith (the dropout) a Maltese Liverpudlian who as a male nurse was very popular being invited to lots of nurses parties (twenty girls to every guy). One time several of us were gathered together to discuss whom amongst us was the most normal. The general opinion was that Mick (the estate agent) was the most normal of our group but even he was a bit peculiar.

My visits to the SAGB continued and I had successful sittings with Agnes Porter and David Young. Many of my favourite Mediums had by this time either retired or passed on. One of the newer Mediums Nelson Ross, who lived in Bournemouth, took me to be introduced to Tom Johanson the General Secretary of the SAGB. I was according shown into a beautiful room panelled from floor to ceiling with wood where Tom was seated behind a desk. On being introduced as an up and coming young Medium Tom looked over his spectacles and said "Young man before very long you will be working here as a Medium." With these words ringing in my ears I beat a hasty retreat to the safety of the café below.

In the late 1960's I had several adventurous holidays abroad visiting Lisbon in Portugal with Brian (the bus driver) when the country was in the grip of the oppressive right-wing regime of Antonio Salazar with secret police everywhere. The journey to Portugal was terrible as we crossed the Bay of Biscay in a force 9 gale. The following year Jim and I toured France in an old Austin Mini doing 2,500 miles in only ten days. Arriving one night near Grenoble we pitched our tent on the campsite wondering why ours was the only tent there. Waking up in the middle of

40

the night half frozen we realised the campsite was in the mountains. Near Vienne we met a couple of girls, I spent some time creating the image of a sophisticated English man. Jim who said to the girls "Will you come back to our tent" ruined the whole effect?

Direct Voice mediumship is a relatively rare gift, in the case of Leslie Flint the Spirit Voices came completely independent of the medium from an area above his head. At the time when I sat with him he was nearing the end of his career. On four occasions our sitting was completely blank. The fifth time we sat in a darkened room Mickey the Cockney guide was heard speaking at exactly the same time as the Medium, proving the voice of the guide was separate to that of the Medium. I cannot say I received personal evidence from the session although I understand that in earlier years his work was extremely evidential. During the session a Frenchman who was unknown to me spoke telling me he was taking a special interest in my psychic work. He told me that I would develop deep trance an area that has always fascinated me and that he would help me with this. Well over thirty years later I am still waiting. Perhaps spirit could see the potential but my natural attitude of doubt has blocked the channel of communication.

Bournemouth has always for a town of its size been the home of more good mediums than any comparative town in Great Britain. Grace Boyers now nearing the end of her career was not only a brilliant clairvoyant but also gave enthralling talks that held ones attention throughout. Her trance work was of the highest calibre. Eve Hopkinson had a fine reputation and worked at both the College of Psychic Studies and the SAGB. Michael Ahearn another first class demonstrator was also a Bournemouth resident together with Nelson Ross and Fred Jordan Gill who have already been mentioned.

Our town also had its fair share of characters. Harris Shoerats claimed to be the oldest man in the World. In fact his claim was entered in " The Guinness Book of Records." One day I got Harris, who was originally from Russia into conversation. Asking him the obvious question regarding the secret of his old age he answered " I have never smoked, drank alcohol or had anything to do with women." My reply was " what a waste of 105 years." However in reality Harris was not, even at his great age without wit and a sense of humour. Although it was true he was teetotal and never smoked he had been married with children. Another local celebrity was Derek Bainbridge who was most certainly not teetotal, his office being " the Criterion ", Longs Wine Lodge and the Badger Bars. A diabetic his social habits were not congenial to his good health. When the worse for wear he would cross the road holding his hand up with scant regard for traffic. He always spoke with a beautiful Public School accent. Always careful not to reveal too much of his history nevertheless enquiries revealed an education at Shrewsbury School and a boyhood close friendship with Sir John Langford-Holt for many years Member of Parliament for Shrewsbury.

41

In my domestic life the time came for me to set up my own home. Although the flat I bought was in a poor state of repair my friends Roy and Jane worked so hard at redecorating. In addition Dad got one of his friends to fit a new bathroom and kitchen and soon my first days of independence began. Life became hectic a wide social life, the demands of promotion in the office coming only a short while after the increased burden of a mortgage, coincidence I wonder, and increased work in the Spiritualist movement.

I was now starting a considerable amount of long distance work, several important Spiritualists centres being served for the first time including Worthing and Exeter [by coincidence the opening ceremony of this church was performed by Sir Archibald Sinclair. Exeter was in fact my first long distance engagement. I was naturally nervous as I boarded the coach at Bournemouth's ramshackled temporary bus station. Exeter itself is a pleasant Cathedral city the Spiritualist Church being a solid red brick building just off the main street. After my engagement the President Mrs Gillard, who I would subsequently get to know over many years, told me that she and the Committee were well pleased with the standard of my work. I have had the pleasure of serving this well appointed and major centre of Spiritual Truth for well over twenty years. The local churches of course continued to support my work. Both the main Bournemouth churches always attracted considerable congregations. One evening after demonstrating at a packed meeting at Bath Road I was approached by an elderly lady who told me I had a fine future as a public Medium. It was only afterwards that I recognised her as Grace Boyers. It was nice to get encouragement from such a well-respected person.

Not that as a young up and coming Medium I got carried away with my own importance. One night coming away from a successful meeting to another packed audience eager to obtain evidence I heard myself in thought telling myself how well I had done only to be brought down to earth by a spiritual voice telling me I should have done much better. Generally over the years however I have been my own severest critic and luckily a number of close friends have always offered constructive criticism and analysis of my work. My mediumship did not always help me in my romantic life however. One girlfriend whilst attending one of my demonstrations obtained a message that was not complimentary. I had failed to recognise her whilst delivering the message, a not unusual occurrence considering my limited vision and concentration required to successfully pass on a correct message. Some weeks later I helped her to move into a new flat situated at the top of the house. So you can imagine I spent many hours carrying various boxes up many flights of stairs. After an extremely exhausting weekend I felt I had more than made up for the episode of the uncomplimentary message. The next week she finished with me. Another girl-friend on hearing of my talent arranged for several of her friends to have sittings with me. I then received an irate telephone call from her as her friends had accused her of passing on information about them to me an occurrence that most definitely had not taken place. The conversation was however a tribute to the accuracy of the information given.

In 1979 a General Election was called just after another Liberal by-election victory {Liverpool Edge Hill won by David Alton}. So the Liberals entered the campaign in good heart. Of course in terms of funds they could not hope to compete with Labour {in disarray anyway} and the Conservatives who won a crushing victory. Regretfully they were left with a total of only 11 seats a net loss of 2 from the 1974 General Election despite recording a respectable 14% of the vote. They also managed to hold the by-election gains at Rochdale, Isle of Ely and Berwick although this was off set by some other losses elsewhere.

I never hid from my fellow office workers the fact I was a Spiritualist Medium. One particular colleague had nagged me for years for a sitting. She did not want evidence of survival in my view, the main purpose but not only purpose of any session, but guidance with her romantic life. Several other Mediums had told her she would marry this certain man. Despite this I thought it extremely unlikely but as I knew her well I did not wish to become involved in the matter. So whenever the subject of a sitting came up I always politely avoided the position. I also rarely see psychically outside the working environment, having made the decision to do this right from the beginning of my training believing mediumship to be a discipline. However there are exceptions to any rule and should the Spiritual world consider it an extremely urgent situation I have asked them to intervene and give me Spiritual vision should the occasion demand. So one night out socialising when I saw this girl with a friend my natural instinct was to avoid her. Suddenly I just knew I had to give a message to her friend. Throwing caution to the wind I approached the friend and gave her a message of a very personal nature. Next day my office colleague burst into my room. Apparently my message had caused a sensation. Her friend in a desperate situation had decided to have one night out before taking her life. It was fortunate that with the help of those in spirit I had the foresight and courage to intervene. That changed her drastic decision and changed her life and she was given the will power to solve the crisis. I understand today she is happy with her situation and left well behind her dark days of despair.

The various psychic journals and in-house magazines had carried articles and comments about my work. The Spiritualist National Union Southern District News spoke of " my forthright delivery and challenging address" and of giving " Clairvoyance of distinction to a large audience." Wavelength the journal of Wilton Spiritualist Church called me the Southern areas leading young Medium and that my Clairvoyance often delivered with humour can provide excellent evidence of survival with detail and clarity. With this publicity it was not surprising that more long distance work followed. A tour of Cardiff and South Wales followed where I met and worked with a very young and ambitious Stephen O'Brien long before he became really well known. He certainly enjoys the prominent place he has in the movement and has talent taking the large meetings often at venues outside of the Spiritualist movement. Although over the years I have taken a few large propaganda meetings I have always preferred to work quietly within the framework of the Spiritualist organisation. The main strength of Spiritualism is that there are many

43

Mediums travelling around the various churches and societies every bit as good as the big names.

No one reading the vast and authoritative literature relating to Spiritualism could not fail but be impressed by the evidence presented by Mediumship. Many sceptics have tried to explain away that the evidence presented is merely telepathic communication between the Medium and the Sitter. Although most parapsychologists believe in telepathy few accept the gifts presented such as Clairvoyance as originating from the surviving personalities in the Spiritual World. I believe that mental mediumship is in fact very closely related to telepathy and that Spiritualists should not be afraid of admitting the existence of telepathy between the living. In fact in my view telepathy itself between living individuals affords strong evidence of immortality. Every effort to find a physical explanation for telepathy has failed. It is assumed that it is due to a form of radiation between two or more people. Particularly during the Soviet era Doctor Vasiliev and others did a lot of research in Russia on the subject. After years of research he was unable to find the correct wavelength to give a scientific explanation to the phenomena. My view is clear, telepathy the communication from one mind to another exists.

The mind should not be confused with the brain. The mind continues to operate after physical death and mediums are able to communicate telepathically with the minds of those in the Spiritual World. The better telepathic rapport between the Medium and the communicator the better the results. It's merely a logical step that if you accept the possibility of telepathic communication between the living, most people have frequent experiences of this, you have to accept the possibility of telepathy between the living and the so-called dead.

The attitude of sceptics always amuses me. At the SAGB I gave a sitting to an American gentleman. During the course of the sitting I told him the obscure Mid-West town where he was born. His reply "gee bud you got that information from my accent." On another occasion I was demonstrating in Southampton and came to a lady: -
Hayward: - " It is your Wedding Anniversary today and your Husband who has passed on is standing behind you."
Recipient: -" Yes."
Hayward: - " He is bringing you red roses to celebrate your day."
Recipient: - "Well you know what you can do with the flowers. He never brought me flowers when he was here and we never got on."
For once in my life I was speechless.

There was only about one other occasion when I was totally lost for words. I was out with my friend Max visiting pubs in the New Forest. Visiting this picturesque thatched public house for the first time we ordered our drinks. There were various sandwiches, crisps and nuts on the Bar that we naturally thought were for general use. So feeling hungry we helped ourselves to the selection on offer. A few minutes

44

later a colonel type who announced "I purchased those savouries for my own consumption" confronted us. We stuttered our apologies and beat a hasty retreat.

CHAPTER FIVE

LIFE AFTER MARRIAGE THE EIGHTIES

My life did not consist of just working in the Inland Revenue and taking Spiritualist meetings. I had a wide and varied social life. Naturally whilst working on my psychic work I came across a number of young ladies that interested me and courted a number although nothing permanent came out of these relationships. Then I was introduced to a young lady who I knew within a few seconds of meeting that I would have the opportunity to marry her. In fact logically everything was against this, Pat was at the time crazy about a friend of mine and in no way would I interfere with that situation. To make matters more complicated she lived a long distance away and my busy schedule and lack of transport was hardly to my advantage. She was also a devout Roman Catholic and was very wary of my considerable involvement with Spiritualism. Life sometimes has its strange twists and turns and within a short time after a whirlwind romance we married. Being a practising Catholic we were married under the auspices of the Roman Catholic Church although at a later date we had a blessing at Charminster Road Spiritualist church, this blessing was a really beautiful service and meant a lot to me.

I have always believed labels are unimportant its how you live up to your principles that matters. It's a pity Religion separates and I felt our union was a test of tolerance and understanding. I have never kept secret from any of Pat's family what I do but I would not dream of trying to convert them to my way of thinking. Luckily Pat's Priest, highly regarded in his Parish was relatively liberal and on a personal level we got along well so that made the initial pathway easier. We then as a couple had the excitement and pressure of setting up home together neither of us had lived with anyone apart from family before and we initially moved into my flat until we could find a suitable house. Pat has never been totally comfortable with my Spiritualist activities and particularly in the early days understandably resented the time my activities took up. I can certainly say our marriage has been a learning experience for both of us.

Spiritualists are forever discussing what constitutes evidence of survival. We now live in a very scientific age and scientists ever since the beginnings of Spiritualism have tried to find alternative explanations to psychic phenomena. Very often the explanations put forward are not very plausible; the explanations put forward by Spiritualists fit the facts far better. Those of us who have vivid psychic experiences or receive an evidential message rightly find it difficult to believe that its source is from our own or another person's subconscious. The problem with pure science is that physical apparatus cannot test psychic phenomena, which are often spontaneous in nature. The whole case for spiritual contact is based on the mind's ability to tune into other dimensions. However the contact made through various channels of communication is largely of a highly personal nature and because the mind is not easily definable the evidence obtained cannot be measured from an inflexible scientific viewpoint. However the dogmatic viewpoint of science is changing, today no scientist challenges the existence of extra sensory perception or the aura. Perhaps the day is not far away when science will accept the possibility of other dimensions.

Wales has always had a strong Spiritualist tradition and I spent time touring visiting Cardiff, Swansea, Llanelli and Merthyr. In one church I was guest of honour for a Transfiguration meeting during which I got a totally unconvincing message from my Grandmother. I have to admit I failed to see anything to convince me that night. Being on tour as a visiting Medium brings all sorts of adventures, visiting one strange town I was directed to go from the train station to catch a bus and stay on the bus until the terminus where my accommodation would be. Arriving at the house at around 3 .00 p.m, I rang the doorbell to be greeted by a young lady dressed only in her undies. I have to admit I thought I made an error until she explained she was a student staying at the house my hostess would arrive later.

Taking public meetings one always has a fair share of learning experiences. When working I am directed where to go and whom to speak to. Nevertheless sometimes I come across situations where I don't want to speak to a member of my audience. Such an occasion happened one Tuesday afternoon at Charminster Road Church. I was on the platform preparing for the demonstration as with most meetings apart from special demonstrations and propaganda meetings there is no set charge but a free will offering is accepted. Alf Crossley an excellent Healer, whose features showed a great experience of life, was taking the collection plate around. A lady in the front row initially refused to put anything in the collection plate. Alf doggedly held his ground and held the plate in front of her. Finally admitting defeat she put a small denomination coin in the plate letting out a resigned sigh. Watching this I made up my mind this was one person who would not be getting a message. I should have known better, during the demonstration she got two evidential messages.

Another landmark was reached when I finally became an International Medium; I worked across water in the Isle of Wight. Joking apart some Mediums put great store in the fact they are International, having maybe worked abroad once or twice. In the same way some Churches in the provinces made a big thing when a London Medium was booked in the Sixties and Seventies when it was relatively rare for Mediums to work abroad. It is as though to be from London or having worked abroad made you above anyone else. Obviously there are excellent London sensitives in the same way that some Mediums of International repute are brilliant. But it does not mean that International or London Mediums are necessarily any better than the relatively unknown Medium who works quietly in the background. There followed a first visit to Brighton {Edward Street Church} where I met that delightful veteran Ivor Davies. The Church, originally started in 1902, had moved to new well-appointed premises in 1965. The Church remains a leading centre in Sussex.

47

There followed a tour of the north of England where I was invited to broadcast on local radio in Leeds. The programme on Radio Aire took place in a supposed haunted Public House in Armley in Leeds. The discussion was presented in a well-balanced way.

Over the years I have been generally most reluctant to get too involved with the media. I think some Spiritualists tend to be flattered by the attention paid to the subject by those controlling the more popular media of communication. However it is misleading to believe that newspaper editors or television producers give space to our subject because they consider the rich philosophical content of Spiritualism. It's much more likely that they are attracted by the so-called off beat quality that will appeal to the public appetite for sensationalism. This idea was vividly brought home when I was called in by a family disturbed by poltergeist phenomena that was certainly disturbing their peace. A poltergeist is a mischievous spirit, which usually manifests its presence by throwing objects about noisily. Throughout history there have been numerous well-published and documented cases that have been investigated by thorough researchers. The media descended upon their home in the suburb of Winton in Bournemouth. There was no question that the manifestation was genuine and the family totally baffled by these happenings just wanted their lives to go back to normal. In my view they were totally incapable of deceiving the investigators that were called in. As is usual with this type of manifestation although the phenomena did not last long the destructive force at its height was tremendous. A large kitchen cabinet had been pushed over and several witnesses had seen objects flying around the room.

A private séance was arranged and an excellent deep trance medium was called in and a carefully selected group including myself waited for what was an unforgettable experience. In my view part of the tabloid press acted in an irresponsible way. The focus of the energy used by the poltergeist is usually a child around the age of puberty. Several sensational stories were run in the press that were not only unsupported by the facts but based on hearsay and rumour. These stories caused great distress to the family who did not wish publicity in the first place. The private séance began, the atmosphere in the house being electric. Although it had been a bright summers day the temperature in the house was really cold, now as dusk appeared although it was a warm evening there was a sharp drop in temperature. Within a small space in time through the lips of the entranced Medium a voice spoke. The communicator admitted that he was the perpetrator of the manifestation. He was apparently known by the family and had died tragically under very distressing circumstances. He was none too pleased at finding himself on the other side and had attached himself to a certain member of the family {different to the person reported by some of the press}. After much discussion the spirit was persuaded to move on from his distressing state of mind. After the séance the atmosphere in the house completely changed. There were no further disturbances although the family for obvious reasons soon moved. I understand they were able to get back to normal leaving this puzzling and disturbing episode well behind. It showed however that a

48

group of dedicated and responsible Spiritualists were able to bring a distressing situation to a successful conclusion.

The Spiritualist National Union now invited me to apply for my Certificate of Recognition as a Speaker and Demonstrator. I was in due course invited by my assessors to a special meeting in Bristol, taking a meeting under test conditions is always a stressful occasion and the Spiritual National Union always demand a high standard of its award holders. However my assessors must have been pleased with my work because I was awarded the Certificate of Recognition as a Speaker and Demonstrator (CSNU}. The SNU regularly reviews the work of its certificated Mediums to ensure a high standard of work is maintained.

It seemed I was now regularly being auditioned and tested in my Spiritual work. Tom Johanson secretary of The Spiritualist Association of Great Britain fulfilled his promise of some years previous by inviting me to the Societies prestigious London headquarters at Belgrave Square. In February 1983 I therefore took the platform on what was to be the first of many occasions in the beautiful Oliver Lodge Hall named after one of our foremost investigators and researchers who became a convinced Spiritualist. A large congregation had gathered and my Chairman a senior councillor named Len Jolley, who had chaired many famous Mediums explained that I was being auditioned to become an approved Medium of the Association. As I sat waiting to speak always a most nerve racking time my thoughts went to all the marvellous Mediums I had seen at the SAGB down the years, those who had influenced my life beyond all measure.

A feeling of panic descended, as I stood up and pointed to a man in his middle fifties " your mother stands with you." There followed a description of his mother that he was able to accept as accurate. I went on to say "your mother tells me that when she was in hospital you tried to visit her but your bus was late and by the time you reached the hospital she had died." Then I continued "she tells me you have always felt guilty about this but you should not feel this way, as she knew you were there." The recipient a complete stranger to me confirmed everything I said. This type of personal communication is fairly typical of hundreds given each week at Spiritualist meetings. There followed several other messages of a similar nature until the Chairman announced the meeting had ended. Even after so many years I never know how a meeting is going to go and there have been many occasions when I have felt I have not done myself justice. However I had felt this meeting had gone particularly well and this was reflected a few weeks later when I was invited to work as an approved visiting Medium. I was told that Len Jolley had been very pleased with my clairvoyance. To have this recommendation from a man of such wide experience was good.

My first day at the SAGB was a little like my first day at school. Arriving I was shown into the Mediums rest room. Nan Whittle a rather plump elderly lady looked

49

at me a little disapprovingly. She enquired my name and as soon as I replied relaxed and told me her friend Rene Keen who she had stayed with on many occasions in Bournemouth had spoken highly of me. Dorothy Patten who spoke with a West Country accent puffed on her cigarette and greeted me in a warm cheery way and we were soon joined by Margaret Pearson and Agnes Porter, both highly respected Mediums who I would get to know much better in later years. I was allocated a room on the top floor of this beautiful Georgian property to give private sittings. Although at this time it had rather a faded grandeur as the whole building was in need of redecoration there was a beautiful atmosphere within. Although I was called upon to do some public demonstrations of clairvoyance my main work was giving private sittings. Gradually during my next few engagements I met many more of the well-known Mediums of the movement. Lexi Findlater and David Smith {who became a great friend} were fine Scottish Mediums as was Tonie Smith always smart and elegantly dressed now coming to the end of her public work as a Medium. Arthur Clark who was very tall with a lovely sense of humour, Joan Mcleod forthright and honest, Coral Polge always friendly and encouraging. Although not staff Mediums I met Mediums of the calibre of Peter Close, Jo Benjamin {a marvellous exponent} Doris Stokes and Gordon Higginson whom all guested for the Association at this time. Also regular visitors where Ursula Roberts and Ivy Northage, it was truly a golden age and I the relatively unknown was now working with such celebrated workers.

Not that I was entirely unknown, an article in the Spiritualist paper Psychic News described my address and clairvoyance as "refreshing". At this stage it may be appropriate to describe how I receive my messages. I cannot say from where my power of visualisation comes from, however there is no doubt in my mind when I get a strong contact with Spirit. I cannot make my mind go blank, I receive a very strong impression and then as I speak the impression seems to get stronger and clearer. Then as I ask the communicator mentally to come closer, objective thoughts come strongly into my mind and I am then able to communicate these thoughts. Sometimes the contact is clear and the descriptions effortless but at other times it is more of a struggle. Often when I am mentally or physically tired the contact is more tenuous. Sometimes I just get nothing on other occasions the information given is correct but the actual communicator more difficult to ascertain. Particularly at public demonstrations if I feel I have done enough and the power is running low, I will sit down rather than ruin a good demonstration. In public meetings I sometimes dislike going to the back of the hall due to the limitations of my vision. However I am simply directed to where I have to go.

Doris Stokes became the most famous Medium in the World. For years she had been a relatively unknown but then through her popular books became extremely famous. At one time a staff Medium at the SAGB she started to travel widely but always kept her connections with Belgrave Square. From time to time she returned as a guest Medium. On one occasion she arrived to take a special meeting with a great number of hangers-on who attach themselves to famous individuals. Arriving at the

50

packed Medium's staff room she was overloaded with flowers and gifts. Gradually the room cleared as the various Mediums went off to start work. As my sitter was late I was left in the room alone with Doris. She looked at me through her bouquet of flowers. "Geoff I know what it is all about." She was obviously referring to her entourage. She then said words I have never forgotten " Geoff always remember you are only as good as your last message."

My work around the churches continued and at this time I was truly serving my apprenticeship as a Spiritualist Medium. I was making a deep study of Spiritualist philosophy and enjoyed this part of my work especially giving lectures on this wide subject. I found myself working at such places as Andover, Basingstoke, Hythe {Hants}, Bitterne {Southampton}, and Havant. At Bitterne I made the acquaintance of Mary and Peter Clifford, stalwarts of the movement. They have always been very helpful and supportive down the years.

In fact I have been grateful to so many Spiritualists who have been actively supportive of my work over many years. Particular mention must be made of Gordon and Kath Saunders and in later years Chris and Gill Hayes (Cavendish Grove, Southampton) Laurie Sayers and Kathleen Luckhurst (Portsmouth Temple) Marjorie and David Jeffries (Swindon) Geof and Al Potts (Bath Road) Ron Buckle and Wynne Gillard (Exeter). However without the support and encouragement of many others I would not have been able to fulfil my Spiritual mission.

As a person I have always enjoyed discussion and debate. It is said that two things one must never debate are religion and politics. Yet coming from a home where there was always free and open discussion it is not surprising that philosophy in its widest sense has been a large part of my life. In fact in the early days of Spiritualism the movement very much allied itself to the socialist principles of the newly formed Labour party. Much discussion took place as to how close this affiliation should be. It was naturally opposed by those of different political persuasion who felt in my opinion quite correctly that their different political views did not debase their standing as Spiritualists. I could not help reflecting how my life would have gone had Jordan-Gill not given me such conclusive evidence in May 1970. I had at that time reached a stage where although I had great sympathy with Spiritualism perhaps it wasn't for me I often wonder what would have happened had I followed my political pathway as enthusiastically as my spiritual, we shall never know.

This Period around the early 1980's showed changes not only towards spiritual things. The Age of Aquarius was showing a much more liberal attitude towards the spiritual. But also the political landscape was changing. The Social Democratic party {SDP} was formed and allied itself to the Liberals gaining a sensational victory over the Tories at Crosby. There followed a lot of discussion between the two centre parties regarding the division of seats. Then in 1983 the Liberals gained a great victory in the previous rock solid Labour seat of Bermondsey, Simon Hughes being

51

the successful candidate. Soon after Margaret Thatcher the Conservative Prime Minister called a General Election. Again the Liberals with their Social Democratic allies hoped for a long awaited breakthrough. At the dissolution of Parliament 42 seats were held {13 Liberal 29 SDP}. Again high hopes were dashed for despite gaining a highly credible 26% of the vote the centre parties only ended up with a handful of seats {17 Liberal 6 SDP}. Watching the Election results with raging toothache hardly likely to improve my mood I reflected about my life and philosophy. It was difficult enough being a Spiritualist. Belonging to a minority religious group you certainly have to stay with your principles. But as my tooth throbbed and the depressing results came in I was rather glad hard going though it was that I had decided to devote the higher proportion of my life to Spiritualism. The time was coming when I felt we could make a real breakthrough and a real difference.

Mediumship always has some reflection upon the society in which we live. Communication in a personal sense is getting rarer. As an example you take the typical hotel, years ago after dinner the guests would gather in the Hotel Lounge to talk. Nowadays everyone just retreats to his or her own room to watch television. People are also afraid to talk about death, to our society it is comparable with sex to the Victorians. In modern times people would cross the road to avoid talking with the bereaved, or if engaged in conversation would avoid the subject altogether. Because Spiritualists are aware of the true nature of death, that passing over is the beginnings of a new life, we have a different attitude to communication in more ways than one. In a scientific age Spiritualism is the only religion that stands up to scientific scrutiny.

In my personal life I was truly busy combining my work as a Medium, Executive in the Civil Service as well as enjoying a full social life. Pat and I had both decided at an early date we wanted children and we went through the pain of not being successful as the months and years went by. Gradually most of our contemporaries started families and although we were happy for them it was still very frustrating for us. I don't think that anyone who has not experienced this can appreciate the pain and suffering remaining childless can be. The subject of adoption came up and after an exhausting and detailed set of interviews we were accepted by The Plymouth Diocese Catholic Children's Society as prospective adopted parents for a baby. The definition of a baby for the purposes of adoption as far as the Society was concerned is a child under eighteen months old. It was explained that as the Society was only a small one if approved by the adoption panel we were guaranteed a baby although it may be some time before one came available. One of the rules of the Society was however we had to withdraw our names from any other adoption agency books something we were under the circumstances very pleased to do.

My spiritual work continued to expand and one of the leading centres on the South Coast the Portsmouth Temple of Spiritualism with its superb facilities was served for the first time. Although the church was originally founded in 1901 the present building with a seating capacity of over 250 was rebuilt in 1940. Often referred to as

52

the Mother of Churches many gifted Mediums served The Temple and my invitation was a sure sign of my growing reputation. My association with this beautiful church continues to this day.

At this stage of my career many famous names were also staff Mediums at the SAGB and I had the pleasure of working with some of them. Mary Duffy a fine exponent, Les Driver very much a contemporary also served at this time as did Judith Seaman and Mavis Patilla for very short periods. Doris Collins for many years a staff Medium came back as a guest. I was invited to lecture for the first time in a series entitled Discussion Forum the subject being is it Spiritual to be Vegetarian. One of a wide number of subjects Spiritualists regularly consider. Much of my work at this time was taken up in training others, as due to a workshop at Bath Road Church in Bournemouth entitled "How to be a Sensitive" I was requested to run a developing circle. This was to operate for many years, in addition to my private group that still continued.

In 1987 it was proved that everything comes to he who waits. AFC Bournemouth as our local professional team was now grandly named was at last promoted to the second division of the Football League (in the days before the Premier League). So under the guidance of Harry Redknapp our modest team had won the right to play such famous teams as Manchester City, Leeds Utd, Aston Villa and Blackburn Rovers, heady days indeed. Alas the fairy story would not last. In the commercialised climate of modern sport our small club could not compete in a financial way and after a few seasons of glory were relegated to more familiar territory. Truly life is full of ups and downs.

The value of meditation groups and developing circles cannot be over empha-sised. In today's rushed World it's all too easy to forget the inner self. A developing circle is a group of like minded people under the guidance of a trained Medium that gather together to develop Spiritual gifts. St Paul spoke with great authority regard-ing the gifts of the Spirit, and his words are no less appropriate now as 2000 years ago. It has been my belief that in such groups harmony is essential and the student learns to attune themselves to their inner being. All sessions begin and end in prayer, the power of thought is so important. After a while in the harmonious atmosphere created by the group those who are attuned are able to be aware of those spiritually who are around them. Of course all this takes time, and in the World we live in patience is a rare commodity. In former times a group of friends would gather together to develop their gifts sometimes sitting for years to develop themselves or even just one member. In today's instant age they expect to work in public after sitting for 6 months. In my view any aspiring Medium should wait patiently for their gifts to unfold. A disciplined lifestyle is also reflected in disciplined mediumship. Mediums should therefore not be heavy smokers or drinkers although strange to relate I know many that are.

During my time in Spiritualism I have met many characters that have been fellow searchers after truth. One such man was Billy Thomas MSNU who was closely associated with Westbury Park Spiritualist Church in Bristol. In his younger days he had sat with the famous materialisation Medium Alec Harris in Cardiff. During one séance Billy's Mother materialised and spoke to him in Welsh a language completely unknown to Alec Harris. Not only did Billy recognise his Mother's spirit form but they had an intimate conversation on personal family matters. Such is the power of the Spirit. Another great personality was Lexi Findlater a Scottish medium with whom I worked at the SAGB. A lady of slight build she was immensely proud of her Scottish Highland ancestry. Her accent was sometimes very difficult to understand one day in the Mediums rest room at the SAGB I thought I heard her say " take a bus to Ulster." These words had no meaning in the context of our conversation. On enquiry the whole context was changed the actual words spoken being "he had a burst ulcer." One of the joys of working in Belgrave Square at this time was sharing the Sunday Services. There would be two Sunday Services one Medium would give the address and the other Medium would demonstrate mediumship at the first service and the roles were reversed for the later service. I really enjoyed these occasions and shared these meetings with many fine workers including Elizabeth Vickers, Dorothy Patten (a marvellous West Country Medium), Marjorie Hathaway {a very well respected veteran from the Midlands} Joan Macleod (another veteran still working today) and my dear friend Agnes Porter from Scotland. I was therefore delighted to be booked to share the Sunday Services with Lexi. Our working rooms were next to each other and between sittings we would often have deep philosophical discussions. Alas it was not meant to be Lexi had to cancel her visit due to ill health. I kept on meaning to telephone her but Christmas intervened and the next I heard she had passed on. A lesson no doubt not to put off contacting people no matter how busy we are, I still miss her great sense of humour and her deep spirituality. Another character was Minie Bridges from Ebbw Vale in Wales. She had a unique style of demonstrating her spiritual gifts and her prayers were so long it was said they started on Sunday evening and ended on Monday morning but many must be grateful for her Spiritual guidance and help.

On the political scene the usual midterm gains were made by the centre parties including Portsmouth South by the SDP and Brecon and Radnor and Rydale by the Liberals. However there was much difficulty between the two parties. By now I had got more politically involved as a backroom boy pounding the pavements distributing literature. The 1987 General Election brought more disillusionment with only 22 MPs. However against the dark days of 1970, 6 MPs, I suppose some sort of progress was being made but it was painfully slow.

In 1989 I shared the platform on the first of many occasions with Coral Polge always modest despite her fame. The procedure was that Coral would start to draw the Spirit communicator whilst I would link in and get evidence from the same

54

communicator. To watch a successful demonstration of this type is a fascinating experience.

My experiences touring around the country continued. Amongst places visited were Falmouth in Cornwall, Swindon, beginning a long association with this progressive Centre, Melksham in Wiltshire, another church I have regularly served and Ystalyfera in Wales. The Spiritual National Union reported that on reviewing my work I was maintaining the standard expected and it was hoped I would continue my work for many years to come. All this travelling meant sacrifices in my personal life constantly being away from home.

Our efforts to adopt a baby seemed to be going nowhere. We had been constantly reassured that as the Catholic Children's Society was relatively small few babies came up for placement but equally only a few couples were accepted as prospective adopters. Several times it looked as if we would be successful. On one occasion we received a telephone call saying that a baby in another diocese named David had come up for adoption. However it seemed he had vision difficulties and his prospective adopted parents felt they could not deal with this, would we be interested. Especially due to my own vision difficulties from birth we felt ideally suited and immediately told the Society we would be interested in adopting David no matter how severe his difficulties were. On further examination it was found his vision was not as restricted as first thought and the prospective adopters had decided they could deal with the situation.

We then received the news that the Society was being reorganised and the Social Workers who had dealt with our application and had followed us this far down the road left, having been we understood very unfairly treated by the new committee. We were then told that although having been with the Society a number of years waiting for a baby, our application having been unanimously accepted by the previous committee, we were now considered too old to adopt a baby but would be considered to adopt an older child. The definition of an older child is an infant of over eighteen months old. The new Social Worker arrived and it was soon apparent he was unsympathetic to our position. It was obvious the new panel wanted a clean sweep from any decisions previously made. We were not therefore unduly surprised when we were told our new application to adopt an older child had been turned down. Of course the Social Worker went through the motions of explaining the criteria for adopting an older child was different to adoption of an infant. In my view he was defending the indefensible. What the Society in fact were saying was that we were ideal prospective adopters for a child of seventeen months and three hundred and sixty four days and unsuitable to adopt a child two days older. Taking into account the long delays that had occurred especially that we now found we were too old to adopt from another society you can understand how devastated we felt.

We accordingly decided to appeal direct to the Diocese Bishop of Plymouth Reverend Budd and had a personal interview expressing our dissatisfaction at the treatment that we had received. Reverend Budd told us that obviously he did not have the time to examine the considerable documentary evidence we presented but it seemed we had just cause for complaint. He promised to look into the position and get back to us. Regretfully we heard nothing further, and so completely disillusioned and devastated we retreated into ourselves. It is of course a symptom of the society that we live in that a so-called religious organisation can be allowed to act in this unethical way. I have nothing but contempt for those responsible for the way that we were treated. It is a tragedy that there are so many childless couples desperate for children yet so many children are unwanted.

Often sitters are directed to certain Mediums because that Medium may have a particular interest in their particular situation. Around the time of our traumatic dealings with the Catholic Children's Society a young lady came for a sitting at the SAGB. I immediately knew that she was desperate for a baby and this she immediately confirmed as correct. It also transpired that she also was trying to adopt and was on the list of a Catholic Children's Society only a different Diocese to ours. As you can imagine a lump came into my throat. I fully understood her emotions in a way that only someone that had been through the same experience could fully understand. I immediately tuned in and told Maggie, I found out her name from subsequent correspondence, that there would be a happy outcome to her situation and that she would have a baby soon. Obviously after many years of trying she was highly sceptical. I still treasure her letter telling me of the birth of a baby girl.

On the spiritual front my work continued. I have always been happy to work in my quiet if unspectacular way like most of my fellow workers you are now reading about. However it was still nice that my work was beginning to get more public recognition. A report appeared in " Psychic News " of a successful meeting taken at the Portsmouth Temple and I was invited with my old friend Geoff Griffiths to take the 50th Anniversary Service at Parkstone Spiritualist Church. The secretary of this organisation reported "there was no doubt whatsoever of the evidence contained in your demonstration... wonderful and aspiring the Committee were delighted with what was achieved." Another special propaganda meeting took place at Hayling Island where I demonstrated in front of over 250 people sharing the platform with two other workers. I cannot say however large propaganda meetings is really my forte although I have taken a number and been invited to take many more. I prefer the more intimate atmosphere created by an audience of fifty or sixty or the even more personal surroundings of a private sitting.

I have never claimed to have any special or mystical power. It is my belief that psychic gifts are inherent within everyone. However only a relatively small proportion may be able to develop their gifts to anywhere near a professional standard. Looking back I realise I was guided to meet the right people, who were a strong spiritual influence on me at the right time. I was also helped by having, due to my personal circumstances, the time to develop naturally. In addition I had the patience to await the unfolding of my natural intuition something I feel is essential to good mediumship. I have also never felt my scientific mind has ever been a barrier to my psychic perception. There is a strong scientific link between Spiritualism, psychic gifts and phenomena and the analytical study of these gifts.

However long ago serious researchers came to the conclusion that the results of psychic manifestations could not be explained away by mere physical explanation. With many spiritual gifts the ordinary senses are in some way by-passed. Our understanding of these gifts have grown and the scientific communities for so long sceptical has realised its definitions and boundaries are movable. My perception I have learned is independent of the five senses. When working with my perception I am somehow here but not here. I often become aware of a physical situation without being there. Although I have trained myself when working to be more attuned than normal many of my most vivid experiences have been spontaneous. Even though Spiritualism still faces prejudice and even hostility from many who have never truly studied the facts there will come the day when life after death will be logically and scientifically comprehensible even to the most narrow minded.

Throughout my life I have taken a keen interest in all sport. Cricket is my favourite passion and I have spent many happy hours watching this fine game. Many sports have been spoilt by commercialisation but perhaps cricket has been affected less than most. In the same way the Spiritualist movement suffers in this way. In times gone by most Mediums worked for at the most travelling expenses. I do not object to Mediums earning a fair living. Before charging fees I went over and over in my mind whether it was correct to do so. When someone comes for a private consultation the sitter does not pay as much for my gift as for my time. That time once given cannot ever be recaptured. Some have the strange idea that a Medium commanding high fees must be better than one charging a modest amount. This is simply not true. I would add that relatively few Mediums charge excessive amounts.

CHAPTER SIX

THE NINETIES

I have always had a deep interest in the history and philosophy of the Spiritualist movement. So it was with pleasure that I was asked to conduct quite a number of lectures of my own choice at the SAGB. Amongst the subjects chosen were The Extraordinary Mediumship of Mrs Piper, The Reality of the Spirit World-Automatic Writing, The Problem of Survival and The Message of Spiritualism. It is a pity that many Spiritualists seem only to be interested in Mediumship and not the history and philosophy of our organisation. Mrs Piper was a Medium who was studied extensively by Sir Oliver Lodge and through her gifts many highly sceptical researchers became convinced of the reality of the Spiritual World. Workshops were now also becoming popular where students are encouraged to develop and practice various techniques to help with their intuitional gifts. My work in London brought my name to the attention of The College Of Psychic Studies where I was invited to several auditions to demonstrate my gifts. The Administrator received communications of a very personal and evidential nature and wrote to me as follows :- " I enjoyed the sitting very much and most of the information you gave me was very accurate." I was subsequently invited to work at the College for a trial period but this never took place.

These days when in London I work exclusively for the Spiritualist Association of Great Britain that has supported my work for 20 years. The SAGB continued to attract the best exponents to work on its platforms including Robin Stevens, Wilfred Watts, Bill Landis and Pat Peacock. Mediumship can be a very lonely profession long hours being spent in travelling from destination to destination, so at the SAGB it is nice to meet your fellow professionals. My church work continued and amongst places visited were Paignton, Leicester, Weston-Super-Mare, Bath and Reading. Paignton and Reading are both well appointed centres and are a credit to our movement. Few realise the dedication of the pioneers who through their foresight and clear thinking put Spiritualism on the map. We owe these people a great deal of gratitude. Luckily many of their successors are equally devoted to the cause of Spiritual truth.

Call me old-fashioned but the way a Medium conducts oneself especially in their public work is vitally important. It is important that our meetings are conducted with dignity and respect. At this stage I was beginning to be one of the more senior Mediums at the SAGB. Some of the newer Mediums coming in had fantastic gifts but not the consistency of some of their senior colleagues. Several got too affected by the adoration of the public. One day in the Medium's room one of my new colleagues was asking my advice about mediumship. Being on our break I suggested we saw another Medium that was taking the afternoon public demonstration. Margaret Pearson took this, surely a model professional for any young Medium to follow. Margaret as usual took the platform immaculately dressed. She began her demonstration in her warm and individual style. Throughout the demonstration facts were relayed in a down to earth practical and sincere way. The standard displayed was typical of dozens of my colleagues that work week in week out to spread the good news of our survival after death. Good solid evidence, open to any investigator to research. I am sure my young colleague left the meeting room wiser than when he went in.

Luckily throughout my careers both in the Inland Revenue and as a Spiritualist Medium I have had the ability to switch off, once work has finished. However in my quieter moments I still from time to time get communication from the Spiritual World my main problem is I forget what I have gleaned psychically and information I have obtained ordinarily. This can sometimes cause problems. Such an occasion happened when I was speaking to a friend on the telephone: -
Hayward: - " How is the carpet man..........".
Friend: - " How did you know about him?"
Hayward: - "You told me about him." {What else could I say}?
Friend: - " I have never told a living soul about him, no one else knew about our connection how an earth did you know? I did not even tell my Mum about him and I tell Mum everything".
Hayward: - " Well you MUST have told me."{Somewhat embarrassed and wishing the conversation had not started.}
Friend: - " I realise where you got that information"{Said with a sense of humour my friend knows my profession.}
This sort of thing happens often, for example another similar incident happened at an office Christmas party, whilst on the dance floor: -
Hayward: - "How did you get on with your special interview for technical training."
Dance Partner: - " That is a complete secret, no one here knows about this but......did she tell you?
Hayward: -" Of course not you know I get these things sometimes forgive me I spoke without thinking".
Dance Partner: - "I know about your gift, promise you will not tell anyone about this."
Hayward: - "Of course not, you will pass the interviews well."
I am glad to say the young lady did get the well deserved promotion So life as a professional psychic has its lighter moments even when off duty.

I was now invited to work at Arthur Findlay College at Stansted, headquarters of the Spiritualist National Union. Like the SAGB in Belgrave Square immediately as you enter Stansted Hall you feel a sense of history. Although there was a dwelling on this site as far back as the Fifteenth century the present building with its magnificent furnishings, including two Adam fireplaces, obtained from the old hall, only dates from the mid-Victorian period. I was invited to give demonstrations of my

59

mediumship and other work consisting of private sittings and lectures. I very much enjoyed the company of the German students of the week. My work was generally well received and I was subsequently invited to work in Germany.

The circumstances of my life were now changing. For some time I had noticed a deterioration of my already poor vision For several years many of my duties were away from VDU's that I obviously had great difficulty with. I had become manager of the Staff Restaurant where I had and was very happy in that position. My own level of performance was very important to me and I had managed to maintain own high standards of work. But times changed, the offices were amalgamated and the Restaurant closed. This meant that VDUs became a bigger part of my working life. Within a short space of time it became obvious that I would not be able to maintain the high level of quality in my position. My vision difficulties caused me psychological frustation as well. Luckily my colleagues were very supportive, my immediate superior Peter Griffiths a muscular Welshman who suffered severe hearing difficulties, being particularly helpful. We had worked closely together and it was said when we attended meetings he heard nothing and I saw nothing. An exaggeration it's true but we laughed at the joke as loudly as anyone else did.

When my problems came to the notice of senior management several comments were made including could I get more powerful spectacles? Some people fail to realise a magnification of one hundred on nothing is still nothing. Anyway the decision was made to apply for early retirement. My mind went back to my original interview thirty years before when much to everyone's amusement I had asked my pension rights

How the last thirty years had flown by. I remembered so many amusing incidents in my Revenue career. The time when I was on the roof in a gale to ascertain the damage to the lift motor room. It was a miracle I wasn't blown off the roof. When some joker tied my shoelaces together under the desk. The many characters I had known, the sad farewells. All these thoughts rushed through my head as I sat at my desk on my last day. At this time no one apart from my immediate boss Peter knew I was going. The Office was quiet and empty apart from the distant noise of a vacuum cleaner humming in the background as I cleared my desk and with a lump in my throat walked out of the career that I had known since my youth.

It was now quite an uncertain time for me. As always Mum and Dad were very supportive and knew I had made the only decision I could considering the facts. Soon I received confirmation of my early retirement and was awarded a pension of less than one half of my salary. I had always the security of my work and although I had worked for many years for Spiritualism in a part time capacity the financial rewards had been relatively small. My first step was to increase my dates at the SAGB who readily agreed to engaging me for several days each month. My regular churches were also very supportive and welcomed the extra time I had available. On the recommendation of David Smith an excellent Medium I was invited to the prestigious Glasgow Association of Spiritualists located close to Sauchiehall Street right in the centre of the city. This organisation was founded in the mid Victorian era like so many prominent centres. In earlier days it was situated in "Greek" Thompson's famous church but was then relocated to a smart Georgian building. It is one of the major Spiritualist centres in Great Britain.

David Smith was a short stocky man of kindly temperament. His early involvement with Spiritualism and how he first became convinced is typical of so many. As a young man in Glasgow just before the Second World War he was training to become an engineer and had recently taken some important examinations. Knowing nothing of Spiritualism a friend persuaded him to attend a meeting. An elderly lady Mrs MacIntyre who David had never met was demonstrating clairvoyance. She came to David and described certain relatives who had died which David had no knowledge of. She went on to say he had recently taken some examinations and he would pass achieving 78%. David arrived home and after enquiry with his parents all the dead relatives were recognised. When his examination results came he found he had passed with exactly 78%.

The people in Glasgow made me feel really welcome and I find Scottish audiences very receptive to both my public and private work. Being made so welcome and appreciated is a positive factor in any line of work. In dealing with a psychic sensitivity it is essential to have this feel good factor. It's only natural no matter how kind people are to feel homesick from time to time. One night feeling happy but just missing my home surroundings a little I went outside for a breath of fresh air before taking a meeting. Parked in front of the Glasgow Association was a car with a Bournemouth registration number! Coincidence or perhaps a sign from spirit I wasn't far from home, anyway the incident amused me.

Certainly in my work as a travelling Medium journeying the length and breath of the country I have visited places where I would have not normally gone. During a tour of the North East I visited a fish and chip shop for my evening meal. I found out the next day the shop was raided by men with balaclavas and shotguns only half an hour after my visit. On another occasion a proposed visit to Yorkshire was cancelled as the church only wished to accommodate me on Saturday night and expected me to return to Bournemouth on Sunday night after the Sunday evening service by public transport, needless to say a virtual impossibility.

Finally I truly became an International Medium when I was invited to and accepted an invitation to go to Cologne in Germany. Still being very reluctant to fly I travelled by Eurostar to Brussels and then onward to Germany. I was met and transported to my destination where I stayed giving private sittings and a weekend workshop. Quite a few of my sitters had sat with Mediums before and many had been under the misrepresentation that Mediums were somehow highly spiritually evolved individuals specially chosen by God. Of course some Mediums have high

61

spiritual ethics, but I do not believe Mediums are specially chosen. I found a deep interest in Spiritualism but a certain amount of confusion with the occult. As far as I am concerned the further away from psychic fairs and the like Spiritualism can get the better.

I had always maintained that I never wanted to be involved with the administration part of Spiritualism. I had only always wanted to concentrate my efforts on to my work as a travelling Medium. I do not consider generally that the two roles can be combined. So when I was invited to be co-opted on to the Committee of Bath Road Church with a view to be firstly Vice President then President I was at first most reluctant to get involved. The organisation had been going through a difficult time and needed stability for a while. I knew my position in office would be for a relatively short time. In fact I much enjoyed the experience and it gave me valuable insight into the dedicated people who work behind the scenes to ensure the truths of Spiritualism are propagated. I was therefore very happy when the time came to hand over to my successors, who had more time and more organising experience than I have. I am pleased to say that in the intervening years they have done an excellent job. Today Sunday night congregations are often over eighty, at a time when many orthodox churches report smaller and smaller congregations.

One of my duties as President was to chair meetings so I had the pleasure of seeing other Mediums work. Many people fail to understand the quality of evidence of survival often given by Mediums who have not sought the limelight. One such message given whilst I was chairing stands out in my memory. Reg Baldwin of Hornchurch a well-respected and long serving Medium was the demonstrator: -
Baldwin: - {pointing to a man at the very back of the church} " Sir I connect you with Scotland."
Recipient {with a broad Scottish accent} "Yes."
Baldwin: - " You link closely with Glasgow."
Recipient: - "Yes"
Baldwin: - "There is a Police Sergeant that remembers you well from those days by the name of...{the surname was then given}."
Recipient: -" I remember him well he was well respected."
Baldwin: -" He tells me he was stationed at Maryhill."
Recipient: - "That was totally correct."

The Spiritual World moves in a mysterious way and further opportunities arose to work abroad, a party of Danish visitors were coming to the SAGB and the President asked me whether I could give a special talk and demonstration to them which I duly did. Through this work I was invited to work in Copenhagen. But never being a comfortable flyer was nervous about taking a flight unaccompanied. So after checking in at Heathrow I boarded my flight with some trepidation. An announcement was made that today the flight was full, when I was asked to go to the desk. I was uptight enough various thoughts flashed through my mind, maybe they could not take me, I thought of my contact waiting at Copenhagen and her reaction when

I didn't turn up. How could I contact her? The young lady at the desk smiled reassuringly and much to my relief asked me whether I would like to be upgraded, this offer I immediately accepted. I was comfortably waiting in my seat apprehensively waiting for take off reviewing my good fortune. A few years ago I was terrified of flying, now I was embarking upon this new venture surely the power of the spirit was helping me. I settled down to a comfortable journey and well refreshed met my hostess at Copenhagen the worse for wear, but extremely happy, from the intake of too many red wines. Luckily she found the situation amusing, Lotte my organiser an attractive blonde typically Scandinavian did not expect a Medium to be other than a normal human being and not just interested in the etheric world.

I was soon transported through the rush hour traffic to very comfortable accommodation and asked whether I could give a sitting almost immediately to someone in need who could not see me any other time. This I did, I find Scandinavian people very open and as the majority of Danes speak excellent English most sittings did not need an interpreter. After a series of successful sessions I was asked to come back as soon as possible. I returned, fitting it into my busy schedule two months later and subsequently have returned to Denmark many times, arriving on one occasion in the middle of a blizzard. The Spiritualist movement in Denmark had been prior to the Second World War very strong there being five Spiritualist churches in Copenhagen alone. Nowadays most activities take place within small societies, young people in particular taking much interest in our work.

It always amuses me when I hear of the Airlines arranging flights for nervous flyers. As a psychic I can imagine, having been very apprehensive about flying myself, all the negative auric emanations coming from everyone and how this would have a bad effect. Surely the best method would be to have a small number of nervous flyers on an aircraft with people that loved flying creating good positive vibrations. Certainly I conquered my fear on a journey from Portugal surrounded by people who really enjoyed air travel.

My abroad work continued and I was invited to Austria a country not known to me. I was therefore rather agitated at the thought of landing at Salzburg without knowing the layout of the airport. The thought occurred to me whether I would recognise and meet up safely with my organiser amongst the crowds at the airport. At least when I went to Copenhagen I had previously visited this city and had fairly shortly before met my contact at the SAGB. Although I had met my contact in Austria sometime before I had forgotten what she looked like. Arriving at Gatwick for my flight I was amazed there were only nine fellow passengers to share my journey. The announcer said, "will all passengers I repeat all passengers make their way to gate 18" much to our amusement. Landing at Salzburg I was delighted to find it was a small airport. Going through the arrival hall I found my organiser Hilda with two friends the only people meeting the flight. After doing a special sitting in Salzburg I was transported through Austria to a pleasant town in the Dolomites very close to the Italian border, finally arriving late at night. Apparently my visit caused quite a stir I being the first Medium to work in these parts so I was breaking new ground. Austria is mainly a Catholic country although in recent years the strangle-hold of orthodoxy is considerably less than it was. After a successful series of sittings, the vast majority of sitters having had no previous experience of medium-ship, with a promise of further engagements I was transported through the beautiful countryside back to the airport. This time as the journey was in daylight, I was able to appreciate the splendid scenery. Within a couple of hours I was back in Salzburg ready for my journey home full of happy memories of the kindness and hospitality shown to me.

Further engagements to new venues in England soon followed a new church or society always offers to me a fresh challenge. Amongst the new places visited were Seaford, Gloucester and Chichester. I was also included in the new registration scheme adopted by the Spiritualist National Union for recognised exponents. Apart from my Circle work, speaking and demonstrating at various churches and societies and administration duties as President of Bath Road Church my work abroad contin-ued to spread. On the recommendation of the famous Psychic Artist Coral Polge, with whom I had worked on many occasions, I was invited to work in Zurich Switzerland. My organiser Cordula correctly expected a very high standard of work and I gave a series of sittings and a Workshop that was successful.

1996 was my busiest year yet, a typical example of my pace of work being the month of October gives an indication of the demands made and the great need of people who thirst for the Spiritual truths that I hold dear. Early in the month I visited Exeter Church, one of the leading Centres in the West Country. Here I was engaged doing a Saturday special demonstration of Clairvoyance followed by two Sunday services. On Monday and Tuesday private consultations were given followed by a Demonstration of Clairvoyance on Wednesday. After returning home for a couple of day's break I travelled to Copenhagen for a series of sittings. Shortly after returning the once nervous flyer was in the air again, this time bound for Vienna in Austria for more work. Once more returning home the hectic schedule continued with my monthly engagements at the SAGB. Sharing the platform for Sunday services with Ethel Watts who in over fifty years of devoted service to the movement must have chaired meetings for most every Medium of note during her time derived great pleasure. Obviously the demands of all this work as well as other pressures were beginning to tell on me. My health was starting to suffer so I decided to relinquish my position as President of Bath Road.

My travels have amusing moments, I often quote the fact I sleep in two hundred beds a year. Whilst staying in Austria I was invited to spend the day in the Czech Republic. Travelling over the border in a car with three ladies my organiser men-tioned to the border guard that they were taking this English gentleman for a visit to the Czech Republic. The reply was to the effect was I being kidnapped or was I going voluntarily. Most British visitors of course experience this Country from the tourist

Fred Jordan - Gill

Grace Boyers

Geoffrey Hayward and Coral Polge

David Smith

areas around the beautiful City of Prague. Although since the fall of Communism the government has made great strides forward I saw so much poverty and hardship. How lucky we have been to live in a free and democratic society something we should never take for granted.

Newcomers to Spiritualism and others are often puzzled what Spiritualism really stands for. Despite much of my working life being spent giving evidence that we, on passing from this life progress on to another dimension there are also considerable philosophical implications to all this. Spiritualists are sometimes however the most self-critical people in the World. Many first of all experience mediumship from a public demonstration of clairvoyance. Some come out of curiosity, others from a detached spirit of enquiry whilst others come in despair at the passing of a loved one. Many times I have seen people transformed through receiving comforting and evidential messages from their loved ones. They have witnessed proof that there loved ones still live and can under certain conditions still communicate with them and be aware of their circumstances. However many public meetings seldom produce the ideal conditions, if sometimes messages may seem vague and lacking in conviction the fault may not lie with either the Medium or the Communicator. The atmosphere produced by the audience is of utmost importance. In my view and I have made a deep study of this matter the psychic faculties are more likely to be exercised in an atmosphere that is relaxed, happy, harmonious and lively. Solemnity is not, as some Spiritualists mistakenly believe, an essential part of our religious services it is in fact likely to block and stifle the psychic flow. It reminds me of the time a young lady came to me for a sitting at the SAGB. She walked in my room looking very uncomfortable and sat down opposite me. I remarked that she looked as if she was about to visit the dentist. Her eyes widened and her face gave away her amazement. She remarked " how on earth did you know I am a dentist yet I hate going to the dentist myself?" She saw my amusement and immediately relaxed this was followed by a successful session. Communication very often works best when there is joy and laughter; God is not mocked by levity.

My work continued and new destinations were visited at home and abroad. As well as the visits to my usual loyal band of churches new places served included Plymouth, Cowes {Isle of Wight} and Northampton. I also received two awards. Firstly the Spiritualist National Union Long Service Award {LSSNU} for 25 continuous years service as a Medium and secondly the Institute of Spiritualist Mediums approved Medium status {ISM/RAM} recognising my standard of work and presentation skills. Another highlight was appearing at Bitterne Church {Southampton} special 50th Anniversary meeting with Coral Polge. A report appeared in the Spiritualist press "a full house saw international Psychic Artist Coral Polge and Medium Geoffrey Hayward. They worked well together with Geoff picking up the same link as Coral within seconds and a good number of pictures being drawn." I would explain that at such meetings when a Psychic Artist and Medium work together the Artist draws the picture of the Spirit communicator whilst the medium connecting on the same wavelength gives clairvoyant details relevant to the communicator recipient or both. It's a fascinating procedure that can produce brilliant evidence of survival.

Time moved on and my enthusiasm for politics had not been dampened by years of disappointment. The usual collection of gains had been made in mid term by the Liberal Democrats. One exciting gain had been in the neighbouring town of Christchurch where Dianne Maddock achieved a fantastic swing in what previously had been a rock solid Conservative seat. Another exciting victory had been achieved in Eastleigh so when the General Election was called I was not surprisingly caught up by the exciting atmosphere. One did not have to be psychic to feel something unusual was in the air. A fair amount of my time was spent foot slogging in Christchurch canvassing and pushing literature through doors. If only Spiritualists could motivate the same manpower to spread Spiritual truths to those desperately in need. The reaction of people on the doorstep is amazing. One man told me he would rather vote for the devil than vote Liberal Democrat, a little extreme one would think. My immediate reaction was to suggest as his friend was not standing perhaps he would reconsider. Few people even only vaguely interested in politics will forget the night of 1ST May 1997. It is on a par with the first landing on the Moon or when President Kennedy was shot. Everybody knows where he or she was on these occasions. As a Liberal I knew watching the results that a few seats were crucial to our chances. One of the first to declare was meant to be one of our target seats Torbay. The caption came up recount, so we knew it was a close call. Finally the result came, Liberal Democrat gain, Adrian Sanders had won by 12 votes. This set the scene for a night of excitement . Of course it was a massively successful night for Labour. But for the Liberals modest success as seat after seat of our targets were gained. Such places as Sheffield Hallam, Hereford, Winchester, Lewes Colchester, Taunton and Northavon had Liberal MPs. Although there was the disappointment of losing Christchurch, the party at least achieved a modest breakthrough with 46 seats.

People often ask me whether with my psychic faculties I can predict the results of elections, horse races, roulette and other things. These days bookmakers will take bets on anything. If the answer were yes I would be a very wealthy man and certainly would not need to work. One day a lady came for a sitting during the course of our conversation she indicated that she had a big problem she wanted to discuss. She explained that the spirits kept on giving her next week's lottery numbers. Obviously in my opinion the dear soul had an overactive imagination. I told her I did not see it as a problem. She did not however give me the winning combination for the following week. On the subject of gambling I am a fairly regular visitor to one of our local casinos. It is a wonderful place for people watching. One night watching a game of roulette I came across a former office colleague who proceeded to predict the next four numbers to come up. He got all four correct and given the fact with each spin the odds on each number is 37-1 it was quite an achievement. I think he must be in the wrong job. But joking apart even he was surprised and none of us had the

Margaret Pearson

Agnes Porter

William Redmond

Nora Blackwood

confidence to actually bet on his predictions I assume that as he still works for the Inland Revenue he cannot do this often!

On the subject of gambling a friend with some intuitive ability came excitingly to me having had a vivid dream that had made a big impression upon him. He dreamt he was at the famous horse race The Derby and he saw three horses pass the post one after the other. When he woke he was impressed by the strong memory of the dream even remembering the names of the horses concerned. His feeling of excitement intensified even further when he found the three named horses in the dream were actually running in the race that was to take place in the next few weeks. By now he imagined all the wealth that would be coming his way. Sure enough the race took place and his three named horses passed the post one after the other, sixth seventh and eighth.

It leads one on to how sometimes with messages from the spiritual world it is easy to misinterpret what is given. Back in the 1980's at the SAGB the Mediums, unless engaged in the evening public demonstrations and lectures, were employed at 7-00 p.m. taking group sittings. Here a group of five people often strangers to each other would gather for an hour, each person receiving a message of some ten minutes duration. It was sometimes very difficult after a full day giving private consultations when you could deeply go into contact to work on this more superficial vibration. These groups often contained office girls wanting to know about their romantic situations. Sometimes you got sitters having received their message would get very restless at sitting through the other participants messages making contact even more difficult. The conditions and results were often best with experienced sitters who booked the whole group with friends or relatives who were interested in each other's communications. Anyway how we dreaded getting a difficult group at the end of the day. This particular day I climbed the stairs wondering what sort of group I would have. Immediately on entering the room I was struck by the good atmosphere and immediately drawn to an attractive young lady who I proceeded to give a precise message to. Her Grandmother communicated and I described in considerable detail a man who I felt was still living, a fairly unusual occurrence as the overwhelming majority of people I see clairvoyantly have passed over. This turned out to be her partner. I then distinctly heard her Grandmother say " this man will be a big influence on her life." I faithfully repeated these words making sure as usual that I did not put my own interpretation on what was given. In due course the session ended and we all went our separate ways. During the next few weeks this young lady kept on coming into my mind and the message I gave her. This again is most unusual the vast majority of messages I give are more or less completely forgotten almost as soon as they are given. A few weeks later I returned again to the SAGB. Soon after arriving the young lady approached me obviously in an irate state. She reminded me of the message that I had given her, which I readily admitted, unusually enough, that I had totally remembered. She then said the words " that man you described ran off with a substantial amount of my money." Now if we examine the message given it is open to several interpretations. It is a pity that a more direct warning was not given but the

67

sitter could not deny the validity of the message. It was her interpretation that was perhaps at fault. But it was an important lesson in examining the precise words of any communication from spirit

People sometimes get confused with the real purpose of mediumship. David Young was a brilliant Medium who made a big impression upon researchers and others. He told about the time that a lady visited him for a sitting the following conversation took place: -
Sitter: - " I do not want any evidence I want to know three things will I move, will I go on holiday this year and thirdly will I get married again".
David Young: -" Well for your first question go to a estate agent, for your second go to a travel agent thirdly go to a marriage bureaux".
I think the advice given was good common sense.

On the subject of marriage bureaux I am reminded of a good adventure from my single days. One of our friends was always thinking of various schemes to chat up available young ladies. His ideas were always great in theory but never worked out in practice. One day he came up with yet another new idea. There was a marriage bureaux situated in Old Christchurch Road Bournemouth. My friend reasoned quite logically that the young ladies using this establishment would be interested in meeting available guys. So we hung outside attempting to chat up each young lady coming out of the building. Alas the reaction from each young lady was not what we expected. We got at best a very frosty reception. It was only afterwards we ascertained in the same building was a dentist. I do not think anyone is at their best with a mouth full of fresh fillings.

On the same theme working in Austria a young lady had a sitting. We got her dilemma straight away her young man had asked her to marry him. Her difficulty was that she did not feel ready to marry him yet but she was terrified that should she refuse him he would leave her. She asked me what she should do, I explained that it was not a question a Medium should ever answer. However I explained the only logical way forward. To be honest with her young man and explain she needed time. But it was important to give positive hope for the future I then instructed my organiser to give the young lady a full refund of her fee. She did not need a Medium but a friend to talk over the situation. There was a happy sequel to the situation for the good couple did get married at a time when she felt ready.

All Mediums are put into difficult situations because certain sitters, fortunately a small minority, expect the Spiritual World to run their lives. Recently I had a sitter who simply wanted me to tell her to kick out her boyfriend. I obviously totally refused to tell her this explaining this should be her decision and her decision alone. Because I would not tell her what she wanted she sent a letter of complaint to my organisers full of half-truths. Thank goodness sitters like this are a relative rarity although all Mediums I suspect come across this type of sitter from time to time.

Some other situations are even more beyond what the average person could imagine. Whilst in Germany a couple of young girls of around fourteen years of age requested a sitting. I told my organiser that whilst I was perfectly happy to have a general talk to them there was no way I would give them a sitting. It would be totally inappropriate due to their age. During our chat one of the young ladies explained her problem. Her boyfriend had run off with another girl, could I please change him into a frog. Some people have got very strange ideas as to the real abilities and functions of a Medium.

One night demonstrating in a provincial church I gave a message to a lady telling her she had recently acquired some antiques and was now attempting to sell them on the quiet. She nearly fell off her chair when I told her away from mediumship I worked for the Inland Revenue. Lucky for her I was off duty at the time. Recently I saw an advertisement for a meeting to be taken by a gentleman who is a detective calling himself "The Psychic Cop." Apparently he takes quite a few large meetings just think if I had been called " The Psychic Taxman" I would have emptied the churches.

I strongly believe we are guided by those in the Spiritual World. However I do not believe the spiritual wish to run our lives for us. I do not consider that every thought that floats through my head and every action that I take are inspired by those in theSpiritual World. I do believe however there are those in spirit who have genuine interest in our welfare. However contact with theSpiritual World does not alone ensure spiritual awareness. That spiritual awareness and inspiration should however grow and grow and the influence of those in the spirit get stronger.

My work in Germany really started to open up, I began working in Hanover, Osterole and Bavaria many having the pleasure of sitting with a Medium for the very first time, truly I felt I was treading new ground. I enjoyed the picturesque scenery of the Hartz Mountains and Bavaria. However my journey from Hanover to Southern Germany was a nightmare. I endured a long train journey where most of my fellow passengers in a packed train were on their way to the Munich October Beer Festival. The atmosphere was hardly congenial to preparing for the usual round of sittings from enquirers anxious for communication from their departed loved ones. Not surprisingly after I returned home I felt both psychically and physically exhausted. Ignoring this I continued my punishing schedule visiting Austria, Denmark and Switzerland in quick succession as the demands on me grew and grew. For some time I had been suffering from digestion problems not helped by a constant change of diet. In particular I had been suffering severe pain with my oesophagus having great problems swallowing. Between my demanding schedule I decided to have the difficulty investigated. The standard medical procedure for this sort of condition is endoscopy, the endoscope being an instrument that examines the inside of an organ, sending information by means of a small camera to the operator.

In due course I found myself in hospital awaiting this procedure. Regretfully the anaesthetic didn't have the required effect and I was fully conscious as the unpleasant procedure of the tube of the endoscope was pushed down my throat. After a period of recuperation I was allowed home the same day. I had just visited Mum and Dad when I noticed a great number of black spots like rain cascading before my eyes. A subsequent visit to the Eye Hospital diagnosed a broken blood vessel in the eye that I was assured was not serious and would heal in a few days. It was however the beginning of a nightmare and my vision would never be the same again. The condition failed to improve and on Dad's insistence I phoned my Eye Consultant. Knowing my medical history he requested that I immediately revisit the hospital and promised that he would pay a special visit specifically to see me. After a thorough examination it was diagnosed my retina, the membrane that forms the light sensitive tissue layer at the back of the eye, had been torn. The retina is responsible for the transmission of light rays along the optic nerve to the brain, where understanding of what is seen takes place. The retina can sometimes be torn or completely detached, similar to wallpaper peeling off a wall, from the back of the eye by the collapse of the Vitreous, the jelly-like substance, that is situated in front of the retina. The part that is detached or peeled off will not then work properly with the result that picture the brain receives becomes patchy or may be lost completely, resulting in blindness. What had happened in my case is the retina in my left eye had always been susceptible due to the damage at birth to this occurrence. Remembering that my right eye has always been next to useless the situation was serious. Whether the Endoscopy had triggered this chapter of events is anyone's guess.

Mr Etchells my Specialist explained that in my case he would treat the retina tear or hole immediately by laser photo coagulation. This procedure would seal the retina around the tear and prevent it peeling off. The laser therefore directs a beam of light through the pupil of the eye the scar produced sealing the hole. This was immediately done and I was told to rest for a few weeks. I was warned should any change in my vision take place I should seek an immediate examination. The immediate effect was that I now had severe problems with considerably increased floaters that would take some getting used to. I was upset at having to cancel a number of working engagements but was overwhelmed by the kindness and support of friends and family. As Christmas approached I felt all in all I had got out of jail.

The next month or so was very difficult and I was made aware that should I have the slightest change in my vision I should seek an immediate medical examination. With the constant floaters I was experiencing this was difficult to assess. So I was a frequent visitor to the Eye Hospital for check ups. The procedure during these visits was always the same. After a sight test eye drops would be put into my eyes that caused a very uncomfortable stinging sensation. This made the pupils of the eye bigger enabling the Ophthalmologist, eye doctor, to examine the back of the eye more fully. Then using an instrument called an Ophthalmoscope a through examination of my eyes took place. So I began to become extremely well known at the Hospital spending many anxious hours being examined and awaiting the results.

Luckily at this stage the retina was holding and it was decided after a period of rest that I could resume my travels and work.

Journeying to London for my regular engagement at the SAGB I felt very nervous yet I was comforted by the thought that I had been given the go-ahead to travel. Something told me there had been a subtle change in my vision. Conducting a series of sittings I tried to put the matter to the back of my mind, perhaps it was all my imagination and another false alarm. In the end I just knew I had to go to Moorfields Eye Hospital. On arrival I was as usual given eye drops and waited, in an understandably tense state for the drops to take effect. After an examination I was told my worse fear the retina had split again, this was a devastating blow. The Ophthalmologist explained I would have been in serious danger of going blind had I not sought help. I thanked God or maybe the Spiritual World as well for giving me the presence of mind to take the positive action I did. I was then told there were several options open for me. My retina had become dangerously thin; a procedure called Vitrectomy may be considered. The vitreous, a jelly like substance in the eye which light passes through to reach the retina, would be removed and replaced with a clear substance probably silicone oil. This would close off the break in the retina from the inside. The whole procedure would consist of the vitreous being cut and sucked out and the silicon oil inserted using very fine instruments and an operating microscope. I naturally did not like the sound of this. The second option was to have Laser treatment similar to previous therapy. I was told to come back the next day, I didn't relish the thought.

Arriving at Moorfields Hospital the next day waiting my turn to be examined yet again I could not help but feel rather sorry for myself. Being on my own I was apprehensive and had nothing better to think about but myself. I tried to occupy my time by " people watching " an activity I especially enjoy. I love studying auras the only psychic perception I encourage outside of the working environment. Lost in thought a lady joined me in, her fifties with an attractive young lady obviously her daughter. It was also obvious the young lady was totally blind and had never had vision. We soon engaged in a pleasant conversation where these facts were soon verified. I suddenly thought how little I had to worry about. God had blessed me with nearly half a century of sight whilst this young lady had not received half a minute of vision. I was immediately brought down to earth with a bump. Soon I was in the company of the Consultant, who was the head of department, Mr Sullivan and was kindness itself. He explained that several more retina tears had been found and he considered a laser could repair these. I breathed a sigh of relief and after laser treatment done there and then whilst I was fully conscious I was told to carry on with life but it was essential as soon as I got home to see my own eye specialist. I returned to my duties at the SAGB and the support, kindness and concern my colleagues showed me touched my heart. In particular Bob and Jean Arnold were so kind even offering to take me home by car. {They had already ferried me back and forth to Moorfields several times}. Stella Blair as always so supportive told me I could stay at the SAGB as long as I wished until I felt well enough to return home. Independent

71

as ever I decided to return home as soon as my working engagements finished. As I journeyed back to Bournemouth by train aware that each jolt could set off a problem, truly I was living life on a knife-edge.

Returning to Bournemouth as usual friends and family rallied round although psychologically I was in a pretty low state. Mum and Dad as usual were extremely supportive. In my mind I felt that if my public career as a Medium was over, at least as far as long distance work was concerned. I was pleased that I had left the Revenue and had a few years doing what I really wanted to do. Jane Francis at this time gave me regular spiritual healing that was invaluable. I was soon referred to Mr Crick the retina specialist at the Westbourne Eye Hospital who advised a treatment called Cryotherapy. This he explained would be done under general anaesthetic. A pen shaped probe to the outside of the eye would apply this freezing treatment. This freezes through to the retina hole and like laser treatment promotes scar tissue as a seal. This treatment I was told would strengthen the retina. Before I knew it I was on the trolley going down to the Operating Theatre. There I found I was Mr Crick's last patient of the day. On enquiring that I hoped he was in a good mood, much to everyone's amusement, I next found myself waking up very relieved after an initial panic that I could still see.

People often ask me as a Medium whether under anaesthetic I have ever had any Psychic experiences and the plain and simple answer is no. Neither have I ever to the best of my knowledge had any out of the body experiences, although I fully believe those who say they have. Whenever I go into hospital I always give my religion as Spiritualist, I know some Spiritualists who state they are Church of England. It reminds me of the time when I was in hospital in Kent for a nose operation. I found myself in a private ward with a Moslem and an agnostic. The local Church of England Minister came in to increase his congregation. After having a few polite words with the Moslem he moved on to the agnostic, who was obviously not interested in being converted. He then moved on to my bed and seeing on my chart the word Spiritualist took one look at me, stuck his nose in the air and without a word removed his ample frame from the ward.

There now followed another period of anxiety, every time I detected a slight change in my vision I rushed up the Eye Hospital. I had several false alarms and felt jittery, as my last retina split had been so difficult to detect. Depending on whom I saw at the Hospital was my prognosis for the future. Apparently although my retina had been considerably strengthened by the Cryotherapy it was still dangerously thin. It was also noted that should the retina detach, resulting in blindness, it would be very difficult to reattach owing to the considerable damage behind the eye. To add to the complications I also have a cataract that is slowly advancing. Again surgery would only be attempted as a last resort. My thoughts went to Mrs Woodford the blind Medium who trained me all those years ago. I was told of Mr Lowe still a legend with veteran Spiritualists who although totally blind still travelled the circuit from his home in Wolverhampton. Rumours started that I would now be ceasing my public work. In consequence I made the front page of the Spiritualist weekly Psychic News with the headlines "Laser Medium takes off again." The article gave details of my troubles but also importantly that I had been given the go-ahead to travel again. So I once again resumed my work beginning my regular monthly slot at the SAGB. I also got permission to fly again soon finding myself working again in Zurich in Switzerland.

During my time in Switzerland I was told of a house in Lucerne where Spiritual manifestations were apparently seen in a mirror. I was accordingly invited to this magnificent house on the shores of Lake Lucerne. After being treated to a delicious lunch and viewing the most majestic scenery across the lake I conducted several sittings and was then invited to see and look into the celebrated mirror. I can honestly say I saw nothing and much to their disappointment told them so. I believe integrity and honesty is so important in Mediumship. Whether manifestations happened in this home is a question I cannot answer.

I was also invited to an excellent Spiritual centre near to Dortmund. The two organisers Claudia and Sabine had sat with me several years previously at SAGB and had been impressed with the results. They now with utter dedication gave up their jobs to dedicate all their time to spreading Spiritual truths. Again although in Germany Spiritual truths are gaining ground many of my sitters had never experienced sitting with a Medium before. My second sitter a complete sceptic had been dragged along by his wife and had no intentions of becoming a believer. As with many other honest sceptics the full weight of evidence has an immense impression. So he sat opposite me arms folded with a look to say prove this to me. Within a short space of time the whole atmosphere of the room changed as I told him fact after fact for which I normally would have no knowledge. Any Medium's work is purely based on results and I am happy to say this gentleman has returned to sit again on numerous occasions and was able by force of evidence to change his views. Due to the hard work of my organisers and the quality of communication my work in this part of Germany has grown and grown, invariably there is a waiting list for sittings and the workshops and public demonstrations are well supported. They have even started their own groups to develop the gifts of the Spirit.

Although on the Continent at present there are few Spiritualist churches most activities are centred on small groups and societies I am certain this picture will change. In Great Britain in my view we suffer the problem of having too many churches and not enough exponents of a suitable standard. However there are a great number of well-organised churches both independent and within or affiliated to the main Spiritualist organisations that offer a marvellous opportunity to the serious enquirer. Spiritualism properly presented offers a coherent and vital religion to those concerned with the problems of this life. Perhaps the movement is better known for its help for the bereaved, the worried, the lonely or the sick. But splendid work is being done in the teaching of our philosophy to those wanting a practical attitude towards life to replace many of the obsolete teachings of orthodoxy.

The true nature of Mediumship is a fascinating one and I am convinced that good contact with the Spiritual World is based upon the Medium's ability to tune into the correct vibrations. Spiritualists are often told before a meeting to raise the vibrations. I believe Mediums act a little like a frequency-tuning device and manage to tune into frequencies, which differ from those, present normally in everyday consciousness. When I work somehow my concentration to my spiritual or inner self is increased but this makes the everyday world out of focus or blurred. The word vibration can sometimes be misleading but in the Spiritual sense it means the many Psychic influences, particularly those of an emotional nature, a Medium is able to receive or be aware of. Usually the stronger the emotions the more definite the link or connection becomes. I understand that every thought; every emotion has its own rate of vibration. Whereas we are able from our position here on Earth and can produce any emotional reaction those in the Spiritual World are able to impress a Medium with these emotional responses. In the same way from our mental attitude we are able to determine the character of the communications we receive. The sitter's mental attitude is so important.

From a person's auric emanation most people can, whether it is consciously or sub consciously, sense whether another person feels friendliness and a relaxed attitude towards them. Equally they can detect feelings of suspicion or aggression. In a sympathetic yet analytical atmosphere I am much more likely to get successful results. Thoughts are not only likely to exert an influence upon the Medium but also upon the type of communication from the Spiritual World.

Throughout my thirty years as a Medium I have always shunned publicity and generally stayed clear of the media. The subject of Spiritualism has in recent years been much more widely discussed than in earlier years. Due to my work around this country and abroad within Spiritualist circles I am quite well known. I have on many occasions been invited to demonstrate my gifts on television and have always refused. Among the programmes I have been invited to appear on has been The Paul McKenna Show, Kilroy and The Esther Rantzen Show. I have always refused to appear for several reasons.

My invitation to appear on The Esther Rantzen Show came about in a typical way. A lady named Mrs White from Somerset came to sit with me at the SAGB. We had not met before and as usual I knew nothing about her. She apparently had never sat with a Medium before. During the sitting I was able to furnish very personal details completely unknown to me under normal circumstances that convinced her that certain individuals from Spirit were communicating. Amongst the items given was strong reference to her collection of dolls. She was so impressed that when she heard Esther Rantzen was doing a programme on evidence from Mediums she wrote to her with these details saying she was willing to appear on the programme detailing these experiences. The producers thought it would be a good idea to have me appearing with her and demonstrating my gifts. Not withstanding that my work schedule would have meant I would have to cancel certain sittings, that I was totally unwilling to do, I was not happy, as any demonstration would be edited.

Clearly clever editing can give a completely distorted picture to any demonstration of Mediumship. As it turned out Mrs White appeared on the programme and spoke of her experiences with me although I wasn't named and she incorrectly referred to the Spiritualist Association of Great Britain as the Institute Of British Mediums, as far as I know, a non- existent organisation. She added that although she was unlikely to sit with a Medium again she found the experience rewarding and comforting. The programme was not surprisingly marred by a most unconvincing demonstration of Mediumship by the Medium chosen to appear. However how far the editing was to blame I cannot tell.

With demonstrations held in the media spotlight the Medium is clearly at a disadvantage for apart from editing the one thing that is lost, that I believe is essential for successful results is rapport and intimacy between Medium and sitter. This must be very difficult to obtain with cameramen and technicians everywhere. I have great respect for some of my colleagues who have tried to spread Spiritual truths in this way, they are certainly more brave than I. However I do question the motives of some who clearly do not have the experience to deal with such an undertaking.

The position of Spiritualism today is considerably stronger in the eyes of the general public than thirty or forty years ago. This is because much work has been done to separate us from superstition. However we need to continue to stress Spiritualism is not to do with the occult. Such practices as Tarot Card reading may have an element of Psychic inspiration but they are not Spiritual in content neither do they prove or attempt to prove the continuation of the human Spirit after death. Spiritualism still does not exercise the authority in society or the influence that it's tremendous message deserves. There are several reasons for this. The influence of the mass media in an age when media communication is vital is crucial. Yet newspaper editors and television producers hardly take a serious analytical study of either the phenomena or philosophy of Spiritualism.

Indeed the Television authorities have consistently refused to broadcast live a complete Spiritualist service such as takes place in hundreds of churches and societies up and down the country. The excuse being the subject is not within the mainstream religious teaching. For years Spiritualists have had to put up with all sorts of subtle prejudice. At one time some local authorities were most reluctant to stock Spiritualist literature. However slowly things are getting better. Unusually enough the Continent where Spiritualism was driven underground for many years is in some ways leading the way.

75

That fine Medium Paul Meek who has the advantage of speaking German fluently was recently interviewed in a very fair and positive way on German television. This is a far cry from the treatment received by that brilliant Psychic Artist Coral Polge when appearing with the so-called Professor Randi. I worked with Coral many times and saw her give outstanding evidence. Yet on producing drawings on this show Professor Randi contacted some pavement artists asking them to draw what they thought his deceased relatives would look like. It was of course a completely unfair comparison, it's a pity investigators cannot study the subject in a fair yet rational way.

We live in times when many are searching for a meaningful philosophy of life. Spiritualism stands for much more than the continuous existence of the soul or spirit. It maintains that we go on to a life of never ending progression, everlasting activity in a new world where we can create joy and happiness. We can sometimes glimpse this new world through deep meditative experiences. To get to this level we need closer contact to our higher spiritual selves. To achieve this it is far better to connect with other like-minded people. This collective spiritual power also helps to develop the age-old gifts of the spirit that lies dormant within many. Spiritualism revolutionises our outlook on life. It desires to create a new religious concept, based not upon the life and teachings of people who lived in the remote past, but upon modern spiritual experiences and inspiration. The failure of Spiritualism to make a stronger impact is because often the image we present is ill defined. The demand for good mediumship and eloquent addresses always outweighs the supply. However now more than ever before there are those who seek divine inspiration and guidance.

The young especially are attracted to closer spiritual contact with their inner selves. Spiritualism is unique amongst the World's religions; it has no figurehead or leader. It has no written word or testament. It has no holy book that is regarded universally as a source of authority. Therefore it in not strangled by meaningless dogma or creeds. It does not rely upon age-old obscure teachings that do not have a meaning in this modern world.

My travels continued and I was invited to a special rally in Sussex to celebrate 150 years of Spiritualism. Afterwards acknowledgement was given to the accuracy of my work. Although still preferring to work in the background away from the limelight several features appeared in Psychic News. A typical tribute was given by Laurie Sayers a leading Spiritualist who wrote the following "for the visit of Geoffrey Hayward the three services at Portsmouth Temple were packed to the doors. Those present were reminded of times passed.... Riveting address and followed by clairvoyance inclusive of full names, intimate family details, and street names.... with a sense of humour that was natural." It was nice to get some public recognition from such a well-respected veteran.

76

In recent times my work abroad has extended still further I now travel regularly to Vienna, truly a beautiful city, and have worked in Antwerp {Belgium} and the Algarve {Portugal}. Again my organisers wrote to the Psychic press and paid tribute to "…A superb demonstration with evidence of survival." However I strive for still higher standards. I compare my work with the fine exponents of the past and I am nothing. There are times when bereaved people come to me and I just cannot connect. I just have to say I am not on the wavelength you will have to get your money back. I feel most upset when this happens.

Some communications come through loud and clear, others are fragmented and disjointed. Sometimes I am really tired and my energy levels are low and the meeting goes with a swing. At other times I feel good and the meeting is flat and I feel I haven't done myself justice. Sometimes I feel a session has been successful and no one says a word. At other times I am really disappointed and someone makes an effort to tell me how much I have helped.

Most Mediums know of their guide or guardian angel. That wonderful Medium Charles Horrey once told me he attended a séance when his Chinese guide materialised for all to see. Charles enquired whether they would work together. The Guides reply was to the effect that the Guide would be doing most of the work. One day in my early days of public work as a Medium I finished my work and was getting down from the church rostrum. Although I have never been a naturally confident person I was feeling pleased with my work. Suddenly I was aware of my Guide standing by my side. I heard the words thought you did well today, I mentally replied yes I thought I had done quite well. The words then given were yes but you should have done somewhat better. I have never forgotten those words. Whatever standard I have obtained in my thirty years of Psychic work I should have done so much more. It's not sufficient to say I have done my best. Sometimes my best has not been good enough. One day at the SAGB a man came for a sitting, and regretfully we had a blank session. I escorted him back to the reception desk for a refund of his fee. Afterwards I found out he had lost his three sons and his wife in a tragic house fire. It is very difficult to come to terms with such failure. I spent many days afterwards soul searching asking myself why I failed this man in his moment of need. It is sometimes almost too much to bear. At the end of the day when I am solitary in my heart I cry and feel so inadequate. However from Spirit I am given the strength to go on. Some people however don't understand the pressure on Mediums to produce results. It's very easy for the sceptic, the critical, the pseudo-intellectual and the unkind to criticise. Most Mediums I know are their own worse critics.

I have given the greatest thought to why sometimes I fail to make good contact with certain sitters. It is all very well to give the stock answer that the sitters critical attitude has blocked the communication. In fact my view is that honest scepticism can sometimes stimulate communication and is certainly no barrier to successful results. However an aggressive attitude is far more destructive. Regretfully society today is far more hard and unfeeling and it is not surprising that with a certain proportion of sitters, particularly the young, who are products of our tough society, I am unable to connect with. This does not fully explain reasons for a blank session. Some who I think I can connect with on a human level still get disappointing results. It is a matter that with some you are on a different psychic wavelength. As a Medium I am aware, especially in the few moments before a sitting, of the auric emanations coming from the sitter. Sometimes these emanations are aggressive so I sub consciously become defensive and closed. Such an attitude is obviously not congenial to good results. However even if a sitter has a particularly negative attitude sometimes our auras may blend because I may be aware intuitively of a sympathetic rapport from the aura. Such an occasion happened once in Glasgow. I had this sitter that I instantly felt I could not connect with. I told my organiser to expect the session to be terminated quickly. As it happened the séance went like a dream and my client was so pleased she gave me a tip.

On the subject of blank sittings one-day a lady came to me again at the SAGB. As soon as she entered the room I knew I would not connect with her, sure enough I had to say I saw nothing with her. As I was escorting her back to reception she enquired whether, because she admired my honesty, she could come to my home in Bournemouth for a sitting. I remarked that since I had nothing for her on this occasion I did not want her to make a long journey to Bournemouth and have another blank result. We shook hands and parted company amicably. Some weeks later she came back to me in London. I remembered her, my first reaction being to the effect we would have another unsuccessful session, thankfully totally the opposite happened and we had a very constructive and positive sitting. Why one sitting with this lady was a complete failure and the next a success I cannot tell you. Perhaps on the second occasion I was able to tune into her wavelength.

I usually know when I am going to be able to be successful. With a small minority of sitters I feel very uncomfortable and within a short space of time I have told them I am obviously not the Medium for them. At other times I may feel affinity with a client but again no contact takes place. Whenever I have felt uncomfortable but ignored my feelings and gone on with the sitting it has rebounded upon me. One day again at the SAGB a gentleman came for a sitting, I immediately picked up an extraordinary amount of aggression around him. I immediately got a close contact with the spirit of his Father who communicated in a very direct and forthright manner that his Son had a large 'chip on his shoulder.' From what I picked up from his aura I agreed totally with this assessment. His Father continued to give evidence of his presence giving his name and correctly telling my client he was a historian, information he could not deny. However the sitter stated he hated his Father and had no wish to be lectured by him now he was in Spirit. He demanded in a very threatening tone for the sitting to be terminated. I was furious not only by his manner but also the fact the contact and communication was valid and correct. I took this man back and the receptionist could see I was angry. This man had paid for the sitting by cheque but demanded cash back. An argument then ensued between this unpleasant man and the receptionist when she quite rightly simply handed him back the cheque he had written half an hour before. There is a sequel to this incident, I found out from other Mediums he had tried to do the same with them. Apparently he was in financial trouble and had no intention of paying for any sitting. Some weeks later he came to a Sunday service and by making various sarcastic remarks and from his general manner tried by subtle means to put me off my work. I was having none of it and concluded a bright cheerful meeting. Afterwards as it is my custom I shook hands with everyone who had attended the meeting. He refused to shake my hand and defeated in his objective walked straight past me. Everyone working in the public arena has to deal with unpleasant people, I saw more than my fair share whilst in the Inland Revenue, Mediums are no different.

Sometimes all of us get people wrong, including Mediums. There is an old saying you cannot judge a book by its cover and that is certainly true. I was taking this meeting at Weymouth when all of a sudden three very scruffily dressed men came into the meeting. One had a face resembling Brian London the famous boxer and looked as if he had just gone six rounds with him. As I began my demonstration I knew I had to go to this man with a message. As with most newcomers he was at first unsure of the procedure of answering just yes and no whatever the occasion demands but there followed what I considered to be an evidential message. After the message he stood up and for a few seconds I froze wandering what was going to happen. He said " I came into this meeting thinking this is absolute nonsense, however I have to admit everything you have said is totally correct" much to the amusement of the seasoned Spiritualists who had been getting such evidence for years, such is the power of the Spirit.

Many people unfamiliar with the subject say that contact with the other side is neither right nor desirable. As a responsible Spiritualist I would admit that when investigating either your own gifts, most folk have at least a few intuitive experiences in their lives that leave a lasting impression, or seeking evidence it is not a subject to be played with. In fact highly-strung or unbalanced people should in my opinion leave it well alone apart from perhaps seeking Spiritual Healing. It should also be remembered that just by passing on a person does not   change their spirituality. So there are those in Spirit who may morally be of a low basic nature just the same as such individuals on Earth exist. The guidelines that should be used come from dealing with these low forces through knowledge. That is why responsible Spiritualists, who are in the vast majority, talk constantly of the power of prayer and development of the human spirit before opening up, especially in a personal way the channels of communication.

Another subject that I wish to discuss is the work of Mediums with the Police. On one side you have those that totally deny that Mediums or Psychics have ever helped the authorities. On the other hand you have some Mediums claiming they have solved any amount of crimes. May I categorically state my position. I know of several Mediums in a totally private capacity who have given the Police valuable assistance I believe this is the way forward. There are other psychics who do their fellow professionals and the movement as a whole no favours by publicising certain facts that turn out totally incorrect. With crime we are dealing with highly charged emotional situations where we have to tread delicately. In fact I am not unsympathetic to the Police view that some so-called psychics are a complete nuisance. However to say Mediums have not contributed and helped solve certain major crimes are contradicted by the facts. One celebrated case was the murder of little Mona Tinsley in the 1930's. Although this case is well documented I make no apologies for repeating it here. This ten-year-old girl disappeared from her home in Newark and despite widespread searches and the best efforts of the Police no trace of her was found. Several well-known Mediums got involved with the case with the direct permission of her family. Estelle Roberts certainly the most celebrated Medium of her time gave important information regarding a house that Mona had been taken to. Her detailed description of the property in an area unknown to her prompted an invitation to the area where the house shown in her vision was subsequently found and visited. It turned out that the house belonged to a Frederick Nodder. Estelle established that he had murdered the girl in the house, put her body in a sack and thrown it in the river nearby. It turned out that Nodder was the main suspect and although little Mona's body had not been found the Police were able to charge Nodder with the abduction of the girl for which he was imprisoned. Many weeks later the child's body was found in a sack in the river as Estelle had predicted. Nodder was subsequently found guilty of murder and hung. Helen Spiers another brilliant Medium also received spiritual communication relating to this situation that agreed with the actual facts. It had a very tragic and sad outcome nevertheless the family was saved uncertainty regarding what actually took place. Mrs Tinsley the bereaved Mother wrote to Psychic News a letter of gratitude for the help and comfort that she received. Of course there are a multitude of other cases equally well documented. However in these times when Spiritualism is given a fairer press the Police have to tread very carefully for if it was known they were officially engaging clairvoyants to help them they would come in for much ridicule. The problem also is that a Medium may get fragments of information that may be correct but in itself either cannot be used in a court of law or move the investigation further forward.

I look forward to the day when the knowledge of the psychic gifts is enough to enable Mediums to be used in this way. My own personal involvement in this matter must in the main for several reasons remain strictly private for the time being. However the involvement of psychics in the obvious abduction and disappearance of Genette Tate typify the difficulties that arise in this area. The Police were inundated with all sorts of theories to the solution of this mystery. Regretfully the case remains unsolved and I hope I do not distress anyone if I say that almost certainly the little girl was murdered shortly after she went missing. For the record I was in Devon shortly after and visited the site at Aylesbeare. My immediate impression was that she had been killed and was buried near to water fairly near the site of her abduction. I do not think it is coincidental that quite a number of psychics have come to the same conclusion. Yet it is clear that Mediums have failed to give anything of real value both in this and other high profile cases. Perhaps in a more relaxed public climate the success rate would be higher. I do not pretend that Mediums have an automatic hot line to solve all problems and mysteries. In fact communication is a lot more difficult than many suppose.

I am never surprised at what happens at Spiritualist gatherings. Taking a meeting at Brighton I pointed to an elderly gentleman. The following conversation took place: -
Hayward: -" Your Wife is in the Spiritual World and is standing behind you."
Recipient: -" No she is not she is sat behind me" {this was followed by laughter from the congregation}
Hayward {Not amused by the laughter and contacting the spirit to get more information} " This lady tells me her name was Ann she tells me she is your Wife."
Recipient: - "Yes that is perfectly true she was my first Wife, it is my second Wife sat behind me."
Hayward: - {relieved that he has given the message correctly went on to give a personal message including a detailed description of the deceased Wife.}
The ingenuity of those in the Spiritual World never ceases to amaze me. The sense of humour and the way that evidence is obtained with seemingly trivial comments is given thousands of times week in and week out by the army of Mediums many of whom do their work either voluntarily or for expenses only. One message typical of so many and repeated time and time again to those willing to investigate the subject happened not so long ago. A young Englishman came to me for a sitting and within a short length of time his " dead " Father, who he missed very much, communicated. His Father reminded him of times passed and he proved to be a very good communicator. As the sitting was coming to an end the Father said, " tell him Rome was not built in a day " With this the sitter left the room almost doubled up in laughter I wondered what was so funny. Some months later he returned for another sitting. I did not remember him but I did remember the incident. After the session he reminded me of what happened in our previous meeting. I told him I well remembered the occasion, but was puzzled by his obvious amusement. He said the joke was he actually lived in Rome.

Recently taking a meeting at SAGB I was meditating before the meeting when I became aware of a lady from the Spiritual World. She told me she wished to communicate with her Daughter, but went on to explain her Daughter would be late for the session. She seemed most determined to stay and I got the impression I would find it difficult to get another connection until this one was dealt with. Rather in a state of panic I began the meeting thinking how do I deal with this situation. When much to my relief the door opened and a lady rushed in sitting at the back of the room. With a sense of confidence I began the demonstration pointing to the lady at the back: -

81

Hayward: - " Your Mother is with me and she has a message for you."
Lady: -" No she is not she is still alive."
You can imagine my reaction, one of total panic. Remembering all my training I went back to the spirit communicator more or less saying what is going on here, help me I heard a voice tell me I am Betty. I then saw the spirit build up by the side of the recipient. I therefore passed this information on. Much to my relief the lady then said " Yes I recognise her we called her mother and we were very close her name was Betty. " In this work you learn something new every day.

It is strange how sometimes messages stick in the memory. Sometimes just a name can mean so much. One day at Southampton Church I gave a communication to a lady from her Mother. After the usual descriptions and personal details of evidence I heard music and got the name of Ambrose. After the meeting the recipient with tears in her eyes approached me. She explained that her Mother was a personal friend and great admirer of the famous bandleader of that name and that my message had meant so much. Sometimes I feel so humble to be used in this way.

The whole question of evidence of survival is based upon identification. What better way than to bring back old memories or intimate knowledge of present circumstances. The evidence for this is built on very firm foundations. Individuals from all walks of life have been convinced. They range from ordinary men and women, hard headed businessmen, students of theology, scientists, in fact people from literally every strata of society. Through the many and varied gifts of the Spirit many have not only received messages of a highly convincing nature but heard their voices and seen their features.

I enjoy experimenting with my gifts and did a Workshop in Switzerland where before the meeting began I would predict and give a message to a person unknown to me before they even took their place in the hall. Every participant was allocated a number at random and then entered the meeting place. The chair lady whom had no knowledge to whom the number was allocated gave me a number. I then proceeded to give a message instructing the recipient not to say anything until the message was completed. Whilst giving the message one thing puzzled me, I kept on seeing a fish. I just could not understand the significance of this and told the audience accordingly of course still not knowing the identity of the recipient. Finally I completed the reading and asked to whom my message had been for. A young lady stood up, rolled up her trousers from the ankle that showed a tattoo of a fish. After the laughter died down she explained that she had only had the tattoo done the previous week. She also confirmed the reading as 95% accurate. Such experiments done under test conditions prove how versatile the psychic faculties really are.

Sometimes people ask whether I have ever given sittings to famous personalities. Of course some Mediums make public that this person and that person has seen them. I know the majority of my colleagues deplore such actions. Not only are sittings confidential but also who has the sitting is private information. If the sitter wishes to furnish information for the purpose of spreading this great truth that is quite another matter. Working for so many years especially in the middle of London I have been consulted by a great number. If they wish this fact to remain private so be it. I would feel uncomfortable in a high profile situation. I have the same opinion regarding mediums predicting national or international events, it is just not for me.

If only I had the time to study all the things I want to study. I enjoy travel so much and my passion for all things historical is as strong as ever. Astronomy has made fantastic strides in recent years. I consider it an absolute certainty that intelligent life exists elsewhere in the galaxy let alone the universe. They have now proved there are other planets orbiting some of the stars that are relatively near neighbours to us astronomically speaking. Surely it is sensible to assume intelligent life exists on some of these. I appreciate some would dispute whether intelligent life exists on Earth. I am also convinced a large planet exists at the far end of the Solar System beyond the orbit of Pluto. I also consider some form of life exists albeit primitive life both below the surface of Mars, alas the Martians belong to science fiction, and below the oceans of Titan the largest satellite of Saturn. My psychic intuition is at no way at odds with my scientific mind, which in turn does not inhibit my extra sensory perception.

Coming back to Earth, and all the political pundits said the Liberal Democrats would a General Election was called in June 2001. Against all expectations the Liberals increased their representation to 52. Even in the real world the underdog still wins.

My work continues, my opinions on politics, astronomy, my love of sport, indeed my love of life are not out of place in this book. Some think Mediums don't lead normal lives. I don't think you get anyone more normal than an Inland Revenue official, although I think some would challenge that statement. Not so very long ago a gentleman stopped me after a demonstration. He very kindly told me how much he appreciated my meeting. Then he added that he supposed I would spend the rest of the evening communicating with my guide. My reply was to the effect I was going out to have a few red wines, for medicinal purposes you understand, I have high cholesterol, and chat to a few attractive young ladies. On the same theme someone rang that excellent Medium Margaret Pearson apologising for disturbing her communication with her guide. Margaret replied asking could she kindly ring back later, she was watching Coronation Street.

Sometimes it is only natural particularly when feeling below par I just do not like taking meetings. One time turning up at a church looking like I felt considerably under the weather, I was asked whether I had come to describe the spiritual people or be described. I did not appreciate the remark at the time although after struggling through the meeting considerably better than expected I saw the funny side.

83

Spiritualists have a grand sense of humour and a lengthy article followed again in the weekly Spiritualist newspaper Psychic News entitled "Ex-Tax Inspector now deals with Spirit Returns." I summed up my philosophy that I was taught to await on the Spirit World. I never started my work until my Circle Leader told me I was ready. I have met many young Mediums who told me they were going to be this and that. But we should all wait for Spirit to direct our path. Tremendous work is being done by the stalwarts of Spiritualism to spread the truth that life goes on after death. I believe that Spiritualism has enriched my life beyond all measure. I have seen ego destroy so many Mediums. I think each Medium or Healer should look carefully at their own standards. The main Spiritualist organisations and Centres all monitor standards and this is an excellent idea, I greatly value the work I do and the SAGB and the various churches and centres I serve are close to my heart. I just want to continue to be of service and spread Spiritual truths to as many people as possible. I hope in my small way I will continue to be an instrument of the world of spirit. The philosophy of Spiritualism is absolutely unique and is needed more than ever in this tired material world.

One never knows what impression a message from the Spiritual World makes, I am essentially a private man and despite my public image quite shy. So when I am in a non-working environment I gauge whether I should mention my professional role. I am in no way secretive in normal circumstances. All my family, friends and ex work colleagues all know of my work as a medium. When travelling often my sixth sense tells me whether I should mention my clairvoyant gift to strangers. Sometimes when asked what I do, I give my stock reply that I worked for the Inland Revenue for thirty years and now I work as a consultant. This is not of course untrue although the questioner is lead to believe my activities are connected to my former occupation. Always when I mention to strangers the true nature of my work there is a reason. A typical example arose recently on a flight from Germany to England. When flying I always try to book in early and get a seat near the wing exit, as there is more legroom. So on this occasion I am talking with the gentleman next to me as the aircraft is getting ready for take off. He asks me the usual question regarding the nature of my occupation. I feel on this occasion to tell him the true nature of my work. With this the Stewardess who is sat opposite for take off joins in our conversation. She said, " I knew I had seen you before I went to that Spiritualist place in Belgrave Square. You were giving a public demonstration, you were wearing a suit. I went along with my friend she is a keen Spiritualist. It was my first meeting and you gave me a message from my Dad. You gave lots of relevant facts even his name. It meant a lot to me as I miss my Dad very much it was so comforting to know he is around." It is at times like this when all the difficulties, all the sacrifices all the misunderstandings all the unkind comments count for nothing.

Today I always enjoy a fresh challenge. The newsletter of the Edinburgh College of Parapsychology in April 2002 reported "Geoffrey Hayward who hails from Bournemouth will be making his first visit to the College as visiting Medium and we look forward to seeing his excellent Demonstrations". There followed a successful visit to this prestigious centre and an invite back for further work.

What constitutes evidence of survival, everyone has his or her own views. It is not my intention to quote a lot of cases from the history of psychical research. For the researcher there are many cases to study in the extensive literature available. My main intention in this book is to indicate that such evidence, so readily available in the past is available today to the modern enquirer. By coincidence if there is such a thing the historical cases I quote now, to indicate the weight of evidence available, concern Sir Arthur Conan Doyle. As well as being the author of the Sherlock Holmes stories that I love he was a prominent Spiritualist.

Shaw Desmond was a famous author and friend of Conan-Doyle. They also had a shared interest in Spiritualism. After Doyle's passing Desmond attended a séance in which his late friend communicated. Obviously wanting absolute proof that the voice speaking was actually Sir Arthur he asked where they had last met. Straight away the voice replied that they last met in a doorway in Victoria Street. They had both run to this doorway to escape a sudden downpour of rain. Shaw Desmond immediately confirmed the reply was totally correct.

A distinguished group gathered at the headquarters of the London Spiritualist Alliance to attend a séance with the brilliant trance medium Eileen Garrett. The main purpose of which was to contact the spirit of Arthur Conan Doyle who had recently died. Mrs Garrett soon went into deep trance. Soon a male voice spoke through the entranced medium's lips. But it was not as expected Sir Arthur, but a gentleman named Flight-Lieut. Irwin. He claimed to be captain of the R101 airship that had recently crashed in France with considerable loss of life. He started to speak in technical terms. "The whole bulk of the dirigible was entirely and absolutely too much for her engine's capacity useful lift too small engines too heavy." Other technical data followed and the relevant information passed on to the authorities. Obviously Mrs Garrett and the sitters had no knowledge of airships and these days were long before black box flight recorders. However not only was the identity of Irwin established but when the Court of Enquiry finally issued its report some six months later the facts communicated at the séance were confirmed. Further seances were held the results of which would impress even the most hardened sceptic.

PART TWO

THE EVIDENCE

Obtaining true evidence of survival is so important for it can transform your life in so many ways. I have always felt of course what goes on between sitters and myself is purely private. However it is I understand essential to pass on our experiences for others to follow in our footsteps. During the last thirty years I have given many thousands of messages both in private sessions and public demonstrations. Tens of thousands have witnessed my work. The different messages given on the following pages are only a minute example of those I have given in my career. I think they are a fair reflection of the standard of evidence on offer not only from my work but also many of my colleagues who work in the same field. I do not set myself up as being particularly gifted or outstanding. However I have had the benefit of wide experience {I call myself England's youngest veteran} and the ability of listening and taking advice from those Mediums with greater experience than I. Sadly with the passing years their numbers are diminishing.

These messages come from records given in the psychic press or details given by grateful sitters in correspondence to me. The overwhelming majority have given their consent for details of their personal communications to be published. One or two messages are from private correspondence to me and the recipient has since passed over. In these cases I feel I am at liberty to publish, as I feel certain I have their approval. I think you will be struck by the intimacy of the communications. That you are being let in to individual private worlds where personal feelings and emotions are laid bare. I must pay a special tribute and owe a special debt of gratitude to those who have allowed me to publish such personal details. They are motivated, as I am to spread this great truth to a wider public and the uninformed. The great message is the investigation of this subject is open to all. Each individual is totally free to come to whatever conclusion they consider covers the facts. It must be remembered however by essence this method of communication is strictly private by nature. I cannot stress this strongly enough. Although I totally applaud those in the following pages that share our experience, I fully respect the thousands who have received communications through my mediumship who wish them to stay completely private. The confidentiality of a sitting is of the utmost importance.

It is important at this stage to give advice to the newcomer or less experienced how to obtain the best results at a demonstration or private sitting. As a rule only attend a meeting or private demonstration with an organisation or individual who has an affiliation with a recognised Spiritualist organisation. Generally avoid, for a private session those who advertise. A good Medium does not need to advertise, their work advertises itself. It is always a good idea before booking a private consultation to try and see that person at a public meeting. Then you can judge the standard of their work and if you feel you will gel in a private session. However be warned that some Mediums are better at public meetings whilst others better on a one to one basis. Avoid also Mediums that charge excessive fees, someone that charges fifty pounds is not necessarily better than one charging twenty pounds for a private reading.

When attempting to communicate with a loved one through a meeting with a Medium your mental approach can mar or stimulate contact with the spiritual world. Don't attend with the idea that one particular person is the only contact you hope to make. If you make a positive and honest approach to others that first communicate this will assist others that may wish to follow. Every meeting should be regarded as an experiment and a steady and open mind assists this method of communication. Acknowledge the medium's statements with a clear answer preferably " yes " or " no" and do not give too much information away. However if you wish clarification on any point ask. You must appreciate that the medium will be able to go much more into detail at a private sitting than a public session.

THE MISSING SUITCASE

Michael Evans retired head of religious education at a Comprehensive school and a Justice of the Peace is a man used to assessing human behaviour and analysing people and situations. He has made a extensive study of Spiritualism and has been deeply involved with Exeter Spiritualist church for many years. He had a sitting with me and after satisfactory evidence was given was asked whether he had any questions. He explained that his Son in Law had lost some important manuals on a flight, the suitcase containing the important documents not turning up with the rest of the luggage. The report in Psychic News continued " Geoff paused for a moment and then said I hear the word Benghazi. Later on my Son in Law went by bus for a break to Tripoli on the coast {he was working at an oil refinery at the time}. When he went to return the guards refused to allow him to board the bus, he did not know why. There was nothing for it but to take a long detour by two buses via Benghazi. Remembering Geoff's message, he went to the Flying Control Centre at Benghazi airport and there was the case with the manuals. No human being that we knew had any idea where that suitcase was however spirit did. The case is now back in our loft."

THE SAILOR'S RETURN

Mrs Asmussen attended a special meeting of Danish visitors organised by the Kosmos Centre. She explained "I am a very experienced Spiritualist but this was my first visit to the Spiritualist Association of Great Britain. Being rather retiring in nature and being out of practice with my English, of all the people at the packed meeting I was the one that least wanted a message. Mr Hayward who of course I had never met before started the meeting by coming straight to me. Being so nervous at being pointed out I found it almost impossible to answer. However with great patience he described in detail this man from Spirit in naval uniform. He correctly named him John and I could not have described him better myself. Mr Hayward then correctly told me that my Daughter {who was sitting next to me} was his favourite. The message impressed us so much that my Daughter invited him to work in Denmark which he has done on many occasions. I may add that my involvement in Spiritualism goes back to the War years when Spiritualism was quite strong in my country."

THE OLD BOOTS

Herr Oberlojer a Veterinary Surgeon had a sitting in Austria. He said, " My Father communicated in the sitting in characteristic style. However the most emotional link came when a fellow Vet communicated who had died under tragic circumstances, He mentioned the details of his passing and correctly passed on the name of his Brother, who he rightly said had been very supportive to his Widow regarding a complicated legal situation. There followed special reference to his Son Thomas who was correctly named. My old friend went on to remind me of several incidents of years before that brought fun and laughter to both of us. As final conclusive proof he spoke of my great reluctance to dispose of a very old pair of boots all of which was totally true and completely unknown to the medium, Mr Hayward".

THE RETURN OF AN OLD FRIEND

Mrs Burroughs at that time completely unknown to me came for a sitting in Bournemouth. The sitting went according to plan and several items of evidence of a personal nature was given, especially from her Mother who I correctly said had passed over with a bad chest condition. However one thing troubled me. I kept on seeing my old friend from the Tax Office Bill Davis. Thinking this was my imagination I carried on with the session. But I still kept on seeing Bill, this obviously frustrated me. Not being able to contain myself finally I said: -
Hayward: - " Look I am certain this is my imagination but I keep on seeing my old friend Bill Davis from the Tax Office, did you know him?"
Mrs Burroughs: - "Yes I most certainly did and what is more I live next door to his Daughter."

Obviously these facts were completely unknown to me, as everyone involved with the situation would confirm. It had a pleasing sequel as Mrs Burroughs rushed home and immediately went next door to tell of the communication. I next got a telephone call from Bill's Widow Doreen who was thrilled about the message. However I also gained great satisfaction from this special communication. It must be remembered that the vast majority of communications I have from the Spiritual World are from strangers. However here a valued friend had been able, in a unique way, to prove his survival after death.

A NEWCOMERS EVIDENCE

Those new to Spiritualism often ask how long does it take to obtain evidence of survival. Of course there is no set rule. Also in fairness what constitutes evidence to one person may not constitute evidence to another. Another frequently asked question is do animals go on and the answer to this is definitely yes. The following message illustrates so accurately that evidence can be obtained by anyone at anytime. Kersten Pfaff was new to Spiritualism and came to a meeting at the Lichtquelle Spiritual Centre in Germany. Her report is as follows: - " Although I was fascinated by the possibility of communication after death I did not really think such a thing was possible. I attended a demonstration with Geoffrey Hayward an Englishman. It was my first experience of such a meeting. I was sat at the back of the room next to my Sister. I was not expecting a reading. Geoffrey said, "I want to speak to the young lady at the back." I thought he meant my Sister, I could not imagine that I would be of any interest, especially that it was my first meeting. He told me animals surrounded me and also when I was young I had a dream of working with animals. I acknowledged that was true, but he then went into a lot more detail. He described the animals surrounding me as mainly dogs and horses. He then went on to describe a special horse and at that moment I knew the communication was definitely for me. He told me this horse had a special love for me and was standing right behind me.

89

This was evidence because I had a very special connection to it when I was a teenager. He then went on to describe correctly the old lady the horse belonged to.

Geoffrey then described an old man that at first neither my Sister nor me recognised because he said he was wearing a uniform. He then stated he was our Grandfather and after a while we remembered he worked on the railway before we knew him. Finally he told us our Grandfather told him his name was Heinrich which was perfectly true."

DOUBLE EVIDENCE

That there is intelligence involved with communication with the World of Spirit is beyond dispute. The following example would give food for thought even to the most hardened sceptic. Mrs Cass Bothwell of Jersey wrote to me as follows: -" I heard you were writing a book about your Spiritualist work so I thought you might like to hear some evidence you gave me in 1995. It was shortly after my Mother in Law passed over; I came to see you at the Spiritualist Association of Great Britain along with my husband David. We wondered what might happen as we both had appointments at the same time my Husband with a lady and myself with you.

As I sat down in your room you seemed quite happy that a lady was trying quite forcibly to make a connection. It transpired this was my Mother In Law who only a matter of six months before she passed over had made me a promise. It was that when the time came, she would let me know that she was all right on the other side. I was a little amazed at first because her Son was sitting in the next room and I just thought she would want to connect with him more than me. Anyway she said she was keeping her promise and everything was fine. She stayed with us for about ten minutes and then left. You gave me a wonderful sitting full of evidence from my own relatives and I left you feeling so happy it really lifted me.

Once outside David and I started to compare notes. He told me he had a really good sitting but he was a little disappointed that his Mother had not been there at the beginning. So I asked him when she had joined him and he said after about ten minutes. I then told David about the promise his Mum had made to me and that for those ten first minutes his Mum was with me. He was so pleased he just said yes that sounds like my Mum she always kept a promise."

AN INTERESTING CONNECTION

Roy West has extensively researched Spiritualism and is a regular member of the congregation at the Portsmouth Temple of Spiritualism one of the leading centres of the movement in England. Although I regularly serve this church I had no knowledge of or personal connection with this gentleman. The detail that is contained in a message from the Spiritual World is well illustrated by this communication given at a public meeting at Portsmouth.

Hayward: -" Were you in or were you associated with the RAF as I have here a man in RAF uniform."

Mr West - " I spent my National Service in the RAF"

Hayward: - " I am being told of an incident involving a motorcycle a Norton I believe on your station."

Mr West: - " There was an incident involving another RAF policeman and a motor cycle owned by a third person at my station. I confess to being a little ashamed for the small part I played, it was a bit naughty."

Hayward: - {with amusement}" yes I know it was." {With a more serious tone of voice} "I have your Father with me, he was not a tall man but has well developed shoulders a well built man."

Mr West: - "Yes." {I may add that this gentleman is 6 Ft 5 inch so one would expect his Father to be a similar height}.

Hayward: - " He died suddenly."

Mr West: - " Yes."

Hayward: -" Your Father is telling me that although it was a shock for the family he preferred it that way. He would have hated to have had a prolonged illness."

Mr West " Yes."

Hayward: -" Does York mean anything to you."

Mr West: - " Yes I visited York a fortnight ago." {For those unfamiliar with geography York is a long distance from Portsmouth.}

Hayward: -" During your visit you went to York Minster."

Mr West: -" Yes and outside York Minster I meet a man painting who gave me a similar message going back to days long ago in the RAF."

CONNECTING LINKS OF SPIRIT

Mrs Lyn Carlo of New Milton who explained in a letter the remarkable evidence she received experienced an interesting chain of events. She explained I would like to tell you the reason why I contacted you for a reading in the first place. One Sunday morning a friend telephoned me and asked me what my Mother's name was. I asked him why he wanted to know this, as my mother had died in 1987. He said he had been for a reading with you and during that reading a lady had come through who was nothing to do with him or his family. However she wanted to get a message through to a friend of his whom was suffering headaches and undergoing investigative treatment. As I was the only friend he knew having investigative treatment he gave

91

me a call. I did not tell him my Mother's name at that point but asked him what name had been given. He said that a lady called Liza wanted him to tell his friend to stop worrying about her headaches. That it was not the obvious, that the problem was with her eyes. My Mother's name was Isabelle but everyone called her Isa all her life.

I thought about this for many weeks asking myself could this be possible, could this be a message from my Mum. I had never been to a clairvoyant Medium before. If I went to this person would he tell me something I did not want to hear? All these worries went through my head but I could not stop thinking about it. When I finally made an appointment my Husband Dave came along and you quickly put us at ease by explaining what you do and there was nothing to be afraid of. I did not tell you anything about my conversation with my friend and the message he was given at his reading.

We both had a very successful reading with messages from different members of our families and just as you were coming to the end of my reading you said to me was I suffering some health problems? I said yes but did not tell you what. You went on to say the problem was with my head, the right hand side of my head {which was true}. You said that I was undergoing investigative treatment {true}. You said they were looking for the obvious, but they would be baffled, they would find nothing wrong. The problem was with your eyes. After many tests in the proceeding month the doctors' actual words were we are baffled.
I took your advice and had a thorough eye examination and found out that there was a problem with one of my eyes.

WHERE THERE IS A WILL THERE IS A WAY

Sometimes a recipient is hesitant to answer a medium who is passing on a message however on reflection they acknowledge the evidence given. Such a person was Mrs Jean Bugden who attended a meeting at Bath Road Spiritualist Church Bournemouth. She was a stranger to Bournemouth being in the area to arrange her Father's funeral. After returning home to Cheshire she took the trouble to write to the church officials.

In her letter she states I attended a meeting on 6th December 1976 the medium at the meeting was a Mr Hayward. I did not presume to speak during the clairvoyance, as I was a stranger. However I would like Mr Hayward to know he gave names connected with both my Father and Mother. He mentioned a timid lady who before she died had to be fed and could only shuffle {my Mother}. She mentioned Bert {my Father's nickname}, Charles {the deceased male nurse who used to sit with Mother and was very kind to her} and Mary Wilkinson a cousin of mine who Mum and Dad knew well. I think I must now attend a Spiritualist meeting near my home in Cheshire.

This proves that even if a message is unclaimed at a meeting the information conveyed is often correct. Very often people attending meetings, especially for the first time, are reluctant to answer. It is understandable that they are often shy, or perhaps initially a little afraid. Some may even have an attitude of doubt, thinking such communication is impossible. Yet on reflection as in this example the evidence is accepted.

A MOTHERS LOVE

Love is the link that enables those from the Spiritual World to communicate. Surely there can be nothing stronger than a Mother's love. Suzanne Golding is an experienced Spiritualist who regularly attends meetings in Brighton. One evening at Brighton National Spiritualist Church in Edward St she received the following message: -
Hayward: - " Your Mother is in the Spiritual World and stands behind you."
Mrs Golding: - " Yes."
Hayward: - " Your Mother has Uncle Harry with her, he was her Brother. I see him in uniform. He was killed in the First World War."
Mrs Golding: - "That is correct."
Hayward: - " Your Mother loved wearing hats. She always wore her best one to go to Church. Why should she be any different now?"
Mrs Golding; - " yes I understand.''
Hayward: -" Your Mother tells me you have been thinking of getting in touch with your Brother with whom there has been a distance."
Mrs Golding: - " Yes that is true."
There followed more information about her Mother's character and description that the recipient was able to understand fully. It is nice to know we are watched over by those that especially cared for us during life.

A MESSAGE REPEATED

During the course of my work I meet hundreds of people and deliver thousands of messages. Edna Brown of Portsmouth told of interesting confirmation she received at two separate meetings at different times. She wrote about her fascinating experience as follows: -
"In late Summer 1999 I attended Havant Church in Hampshire with my friend Pat Blandford who had introduced me to Spiritualism only three years ago. The demon-

93

strator was Geoffrey Hayward and during the clairvoyant session he came to me saying that my Mother was with me. He described her passing exactly, how I had been there to help her. He also explained that my personal circumstances were difficult at that particular time in my life. My Mother thanked me for what I had done despite everything.

On 30th August 2000 I was at the Portsmouth Temple of Spiritualism again accompanied by my friend Pat.
Once more Mr Hayward was demonstrating and came to me saying my Mother was with me. He went on to relay almost word for word exactly the same message I had previously received at Havant Church.
My friend Pat confirmed this and of course there is no way that he could have remembered what he told me previously. I thought I should have told him at the time but I did not like to, as I am new to the Movement. I confirm Geoffrey and I had never met before my attendance at Havant Church and there is no way in which he could have possibly known the detailed message he gave me from my Mother. Although a comparative newcomer to Spiritualism life after death has been proven to me so early and for this I feel very privileged."

UNAWARE OF A PASSING

Joanne Kelly is an experienced researcher who has made a deep and detailed study of Spiritual matters. She has written a delightful book " Messages From Michael " telling of her search for evidence. She has sat with many mediums and has received wonderful evidence. Her book proves the point that I make that there are a great number of mediums today {and not only the big names}are consistently producing evidence. She has sat with me a number of times at the Spiritualist Association of Great Britain. The sitting now described discounts the old theory that Mediumship is simply telepathy. In April 1994 Joanne came into my room at the SAGB: -
Hayward: -" As you walk in this room your Father walks in with you."
Joanne: - " Yes".
Hayward: - " Your Father is very anxious to contact you he has recently found an older Brother who has recently passed over to the World of Spirit ".
Joanne: - " I do not understand this.".
However two days later I had a call from America confirming that my Uncle his Brother had passed over.
Hayward: - " Dad says hello to your Brother Richard."
Joanne: - " Actually Richard is my Brother in Law."
Hayward: - " Your Father says Mum is a little frail you need more of a social life he is talking about you going to the theatre and opera."

Joanne: - " I understand about Mum and have not only just been to the theatre but just purchased tickets for the opera."
Hayward: - " There is a Canadian connection with you. I want to go to the Michigan/ Canadian border."
Joanne: - " I live in Michigan just a few miles from the Canadian border."

A SON RETURNS

Perhaps the biggest tragedy is the loss of a child. It is my belief that regular contact with the Spirit not only helps the mourner but also helps the adjustment of those in the Spiritual World. The more one sits the closer the Spiritual contact. Joanne Kelly has received great comfort from her communications with her Son, for the mutual benefit of both. Her sitting with me is typical of the wealth of evidence when an experienced sitter has a private consultation with a trained Medium.

Hayward: - " You have been making considerable progress in coming to terms with certain things that have happened. You still need to cry and sit and meditate with the spiritual. You have come through a really difficult time. No one can undo what has happened you have a Son in the Spirit."

Joanne: - " Yes."

Hayward: - " Your Son had an accident."

Joanne: - " That is true."

Hayward: - " Your Son tells me you will see the light at the end of the tunnel. You will get a lot of inner strength from the Spiritual World. Your Son was here one minute gone the next, he was catapulted into spirit. The accident was not his fault, your Son has a boyish face a lovely smile."

Joanne; - " That is all true. "

Hayward: - " He was driving at the time of the accident."

Joanne: - " Yes "

Hayward: -" He is talking about his golf clubs he has them with him. There was a bend in the road and someone came into him a larger vehicle, there was a severe impact."

Joanne: - " I understand all of that."

Hayward: - " He was good at so many things in his life. He crammed a lot in, he put 110% into everything."

Joanne: - " Yes."

Hayward: - " Someone left behind has changed her hairstyle."

Joanne: - " That is his Wife."

Hayward: - " She misses him tremendously but puts on a brave face."

Joanne: - " Yes."

Hayward: - " Your Grandmother is here, you have a spiritual destiny, and that destiny is to do with your spiritual work. She says your Mother and you do not see eye to eye always she has no comprehension of spiritual matters. Dad was a spiritual man but in a different way, he was a very gentle and good man. "

Joanne: -" That is all correct."

Hayward: - " You are writing a book with a spiritual theme, You also have a feel for poetry, put some in a book. You are coming out of the worse period of your life. Your Son keeps on saying Michael Michael. He is sending special love to Michael. The world of spirit is not unrelated to this world. The other driver was on the wrong side of the road; he was also travelling too fast and lost control right after coming around the bend. That guy lost control and went into Michael "{said with a rising tone of excitement in my speech}.

Joanne: - " I confirm everything is correct."

The sitting took place before the publication of Joanne's book of which I at that time had no knowledge. She explained afterwards that Michael was the name of both her Son and his Son and yes she did go on to put some poetry in a book.

Such detailed messages refute the charge from sceptics that messages are vague and contradictory in nature.

BIRTHDAYS REMEMBERED

Sometimes it is the intimate but seemingly trivial items of evidence that are given that are important. Mrs Elsie Smith is a veteran Spiritualist who regularly attends public meetings at the SAGB. After receiving a message detailing her Mother's painful passing with cancer and having her Father described in detail both in character and appearance she received the following: -

Hayward: - " Your Mother tells me that you and I share something."

Mrs Smith: - " What is that?" {Obviously puzzled}

Hayward: - "Your birthday is the same day as mine 18 th March."

Mrs Smith: - " Yes that is correct."

Hayward: - " Your Mother also tells me her birthday was one day earlier on 17th March."

Mrs Smith: - "Yes it was."

THE SECRET RING

When Janet Biggs attended a demonstration of clairvoyance at Hythe {Kent} Spiritualist Church she did not dream that a secret only known to her and one other would be revealed by her Father communicating from Spirit. She explained that she was very fortunate to receive evidential messages from her Father and Grandmother. Other friends referred to were Mrs Parker {known as Nosy Parker because she knew everyone's business} and Sam Young {her Father's friend}.

Her Grandmother then referred to the fact that her Mother's spectacles were wrong for her. Her Mum went to the optician the following Monday who confirmed the wrong lens had been put in. The final item of evidence was as follows: -
Hayward: - " You have been looking for an item of jewellery this is a secret but your Father is very happy about this. Only you and the person you were with knows of your plans."
Janet Biggs: - " Yes."
Afterwards the recipient wrote to me explaining that she and her partner had only that day been looking at engagement rings but had told no one of their plans.

A GRANDMOTHER STILL GUIDES

That we are guided by Spiritual beings is a very comforting thought. But as well as watching over and guiding {but not interfering with} our material path with good practical advice they are also interested in our Spiritual pathway and gifts. When Helen Avery attended the Glasgow Association of Spiritualists she was not expecting a message: -
Hayward: - " I have your Grandmother here with me. She is your Mother's Mother. Let me describe her, she is around five foot five inches in height, she is slim in the build. She walked with a stick."
Helen Avery: - " Actually that is my Father's Mother."
Hayward: - " Well she has a motherly protective feeling towards you. She wants you to know she always spoke her mind and she wants you to listen to her. Your Grandmother was always honest and truthful so do not doubt yourself. You have the ability to do healing, you should seek to develop these gifts within you."

The message is interesting for several reasons. The error in the fact that it was Grandmother on Father's side was an error of interpretation. This can sometimes happen no Medium is infallible. Obviously the motherly feeling of the communicator was relevant here Afterwards Helen Avery told me the message was highly significant to her situation. She understood the communication exactly and she takes after her Grandmother so much . She often senses and feels her Grandmother around. You will note that the potential of healing was mentioned. But I spoke that she should develop her inner self first before considering developing this ability. It is her free will whether she wishes to do this.

A SCEPTICS EVIDENCE

I am often asked if someone does not believe in life after death whether it effects their ability to communicate once they have passed over. Mrs Judith Lambert of

97

Dorset often spoke to her Father in Law, who was a complete non-believer, on these matters. Nothing she could say or do would convince him otherwise. One particular Saturday afternoon, unbeknown to anyone they had their last chat together. As they parted Judith said to him " I don't expect it to be as bad as you think." Four days later her Father in Law died suddenly with a heart attack.

Mrs Lambert booked a private sitting with me. She explained the clear evidence from him as follows: -
When I went to Geoff he said to me that he had my Father in Law with him. He described him exactly and the nature of his passing. Then he said, "Before your Father in Law says anything he wants me to tell you that it's not as bad as he thought." These were my very last words to him. Then he told me to eat an apple a day. He was so set on this routine when he was here. Geoff also told me that my Husband had recently had a cholesterol test and that when the results came through they would be high. When the results came through a few days later they confirmed what had been said. The next part of the message was also highly relevant: -
Hayward: - " I have Sam or Sammy here, it is not a person but a black and white cat . He is very small and regretfully did not live to an old age. "I loved that little creature and it brought me a lot of happiness that he had continued his existence.

A MEMORY RECALLED

Researchers often ponder the true nature of the life hereafter. One thing is certain we go on with our memory and personality intact. Ruth Rankin of Renfrewshire attended a public demonstration of clairvoyance at the Glasgow Association of Spiritualists.
Hayward: - " Your Father is with you from spirit he was exceptionally good with his hands. He was also really good at decorating and was a marvellous gardener who took a lot of time and trouble over everything.
Ms Rankin: - " Yes that is all correct."
Hayward: -"You have a great love of music and a natural ability to dance well. You adored listening to music on the radio when you were young, it was your favourite pastime."
Ms Rankin: - " Yes"
Hayward: - " Your Father tells me he built a Radio Crystal Set"
Ms Rankin: -" I do not remember this."
The recipient thought the last part of the message was inaccurate. However she contacted her Sister who is some years older than her. Her Sister was able to confirm the evidence given. Her Father had indeed built a Crystal Set some years before Ms Rankin was born.

A SUBSTITUTE MUM AND A NEW JOB

Often those that are sceptical say why don't Mediums ever give surnames. The simple answer is they do and it is not only Smith and Jones. Jenny Mcrae of Devon had several sittings. One or two stand out in the memory.

Hayward: -" I see a bungalow." {There followed a very detailed description}.

Ms Mcrae: -" I understand everything."

Hayward: - " In fact outside the bungalow is a telegraph pole."

Ms Mcrae: -" Yes."

Hayward: - " I get the name Joan Attenborough".

Ms Mcrae: - " Yes."

Afterwards she explained to me that she had loved Joan dearly. She passed over at 64 years of age and had been a substitute Mum.

Sometimes it is important for mediums to give exactly what they get. This is illustrated perfectly by this next message: -

Hayward: - " I cannot understand this they are saying you are going for an interview But that you are having an interview in the east for a job in the west."

Ms Mcrae: - " But I understand this, I am being interviewed in Portsmouth for a job in Devon."

A SENTIMENTAL ATTACHMENT

We are in so many ways sentimental. The knowledge of those in the Spiritual World of what we do, the intimacy of the communication confirms that genuine contact can be made. Frau Silke a newcomer to Spiritualism was thrilled by contacts made at the Lichtquelle Spiritual Centre near Dortmund in Germany.

Hayward: - " There is a lady here telling me she is Auntie Else she is very close and watches over your family."

Recipient: - " Yes she was my Mother's Auntie."

Hayward: - " She is exceptionally close to your Daughter."

Recipient: - " I have a Daughter."

Hayward: - " She tells me that there is a really special connection that pleases your Aunt very much. She tells me your Daughter is named after her, she is so happy about this.

Recipient: - "You are correct her actual name is Elisa but my Husband calls her Else."

Hayward: - " But Auntie Else is taking so much interest in Mum and Dad she is talking about breeding dogs but it is not entirely clear to me."

Recipient: - " I have no knowledge of this."

Later the sitter checked with her Mum and Dad. They confirmed that when they were young they had both wanted to breed dogs but had been discouraged from doing it.

CONFIRMATION OF A PASSING

Newcomers to Spiritualism and others sometimes wonder whether I am able to see bad things ahead. Some have even asked me if I can tell when someone will pass over. The answer is of course no I do not know any more than anyone else does. However I can warn people to change their lifestyle but everyone has free will. I know that some Mediums would disagree with me but I believe everyone has an allotted life span. However we can shorten that life span by misuse.

Sometimes a life can naturally come to an end at a young age through illness and this is terribly difficult to accept. Michael McCafferty was tremendously brave when he booked a private sitting at the Glasgow Association on 7th September 1996. His Wife was dangerously ill and not expected to survive. Obviously no mention of this was made to the medium.
Hayward: - {at the end of the sitting} " They are talking about your Wife."
Mr McCafferty: - " Yes".
Hayward: - " Who is Veronica."
Mr McCafferty: - " That is my Wife's name."
Hayward: - " She has severe respiratory problems."
Mr McCafferty: -"That is not the condition she is suffering from at the moment."
Sadly the very next morning Veronica passed over. The Death Certificate was marked " Respiratory Failure."
Spirit was obviously more aware of the situation than the Sitter. Time and time again mediums give details considered incorrect but later are confirmed as accurate.

FAMILY CONNECTIONS AND NELSON THE ONE EYED CAT

How strong are the ties of family relationships. There is strong evidence that family ties continue in the Spiritual World. As well as the obvious connection with us on Earth they wish to surround themselves with family friends and even animals where love is the affinity that holds everything together.

Mrs Valentia Baddoo is a regular visitor to the Spiritualist Association of Great Britain. She has recorded quite a number of her messages. Here are details of evidence she has obtained that has convinced her totally of the reality of contact with the so-called dead.
Hayward: - "Your Mother is in the Spirit World."
Mrs Baddoo: - "Yes."
Hayward: - " She has communicated on many occasions and brings your Father who rarely communicates. So today your Father will have a lot to say. He tells me he loved music particularly jazz his favourite being Louis Armstrong."
Mrs Baddoo: - " Yes I understand."
Hayward: - " Your Father is tall around my height and around my build. He was a nice looking man short grey hair, moustache, he lived in Ghana."

Mrs Baddoo: - " Yes."
Hayward: - " He talks of Charles who is with him. Who is Charles is he your Brother or your Father's?"
Mrs Baddoo: - " Charles is my Brother."
Hayward: - " Well Charles is passed over and is with your Father and Mother. He used to pull your hair when you were a girl."
Mrs Baddoo {laughing}: - " Yes I remember that so well."
Hayward: - " They are all together now, however your Mother does not want to be left out. She says she has Nelson the cat with her."
Mrs Baddoo: - " I loved him so much."
Hayward: - " He was called Nelson because he only had one eye."
Mrs Baddoo {with some amusement}: - " Yes that is true."

You can well understand reading this narrative that Spiritualist meetings are not dull dismal affairs. The reunion with loved ones often brings laughter and joy at happy memories recalled.

A MOTHERS RING

Some investigators are puzzled how a Medium is able to communicate with those in the Spiritual World who when here had either a poor command of the language of the Medium or no knowledge whatsoever. Of course the communication is telepathic so there is no need for language. There have been occasions however when I have conveyed foreign words or a phrase that have been evidential.

I have been to meetings where the Medium seems to have a conversation with the unseen. I have even heard Spiritualists say this one and that one are marvellous, they talk to Spirit. I find such displays unnecessary and misleading.

Katrine Pederson had a private sitting in Denmark and recorded the following interesting results : -
Hayward: - "You have a ring. Your not wearing it now, it is too big for you. This ring belonged to your Mother. Let me describe it, the ring is plain with no stones and it is engraved."
Katrine: - "Yes it is my Mother's ring, I have been worried recently to wear it"
Hayward: - "Yes your Mother is aware of this. She is saying if you get it altered in size so that it is smaller you will be able to wear it."
Katrine explained after the sitting she had felt guilty about not wearing the ring. My message would spur her into action. She now wears the ring and because of this feels her spiritual connection with her Mum closer. Some would consider this message mundane and trivial but to the sitter it proved her Mum had been around her. Such feelings are anything but mundane and trivial.

CHILDREN HERE AND HEREAFTER

Many sitters come to a Medium because they are heartbroken. The loss of a child can be totally devastating and the orthodox church, with respect can only offer faith, that at such times seems empty and inadequate We also worry about our children here and it is comforting to know we are being watched over. Mrs McFarlane is one such bereaved mother who came for sittings in April and September 2000. As always I knew nothing about her or her circumstances.

Hayward: -"You have a child, a Daughter, in the Spiritual World."

Mrs McFarlane: -"Yes."

Hayward: -" I feel a terrible pain in the head then I hear a loud bang, did she have an accident?"

Mrs McFarlane: - "No."

Hayward: - Your Daughter's passing over was a terrible shock, she had hardly ever been ill . She died before the bang, she died in bed."

Mrs McFarlane: - "All your statements are totally correct."

Hayward: -"You had an especially close relationship. Your Mother and Father should never have been together, without your Father your Mother would have been totally different. That is why you were totally determined to have such a close connection with your Daughter, as your Mother and you were not close."

Mrs McFarlane: -" That is all so true".

At the later sitting the Daughter expressed her concerns about her Brother who had not been referred to at the earlier session.

Hayward: - " Your Daughter talks about her Brother, her youngest Brother, she sends a lot of love to his partner she likes them both such a lot."

Mrs McFarlane: - " I understand this."

Hayward: - " She says her Brother works far too hard."

Mrs McFarlane: - "That is true."

Then followed intimate relationship details all verified by Mrs McFarlane as correct. Although she gave me permission {as the other sitters have} to quote the full details on this occasion I feel her privacy should be respected.

Mrs McFarlane: - " Can you answer me a direct question, what was my Daughter's favourite animal."

Hayward: - "I cannot necessarily do that, this method of communication is not easy and I never guess, however I am puzzled. I see lots of stuffed toys, did she have lots of animals?"

Mrs McFarlane: - "Yes cuddly toys."

Hayward: - " I see lots of these cuddly toys, I see a panda."

Mrs McFarlane: -" That was her favourite animal."

WE ARE WATCHED OVER

Mrs E A Simpson was in a right state. There is a law in life, if one thing goes wrong everything goes wrong. It started with a mundane job done thousands of times. Having completed the washing up she was putting away the knives and forks. The drawer was packed solid too solid, she had been promising to clear the drawer out for months. In a rage she slammed the drawer catching her hand, and swore to get the drawer sorted out.

Imagine her surprise, a few weeks later attending a Spiritualist meeting she was told of the incident, the words she spoke to herself being repeated word by word. She states "Through Geoffrey Hayward my Mother told me she was with me at this time." Help was also given on certain intimate family problems. Not only was the nature of the problem correctly highlighted but also the advice given and taken was totally correct given the circumstances.

IDENTIFICATION PROVED

Communication with the Spiritual is all about proof of identity. Mr Eric Amey of Swindon certainly received evidence of identity one night at Swindon Spiritualist Church a very fine centre. After several initial remarks that were understood further communication took place: -

Hayward: - "There are a number of people from the Spiritual World but your Father in particular is very much in evidence. In some ways you would be pleased to hear from your Father. However in other ways you would be a little surprised that he is the one person I have firstly seen with you."

Mr Amey: - "Yes."

Hayward: - "You know your Father wasn't the easiest person to communicate with when he was alive."

Mr Amey: - "That's true."

Hayward: - "And he could be tough."

Mr Amey: - "Yes."

Hayward: - "And he was tough with you there is no question about that. But your Father himself had a very tough and difficult life. As much as anything else your experiences with your Father gave you the background that has kept you in good stead down all these years. It has helped you roll up your sleeves and deal with the situations that have been around."

Mr Amey: - "Yes that is true."

Hayward: - "There were times in your childhood when your Father tried to push you too hard and he now appreciates that he tried to push you too hard. In the intervening years you have known the reason for this."

Mr Amey: -" Yes I do."

Hayward: - "Your Father passed quickly very unexpectedly. He did not believe in this and was a cynical man, he is talking about Mr White, a foreman, you knew him." Mr Amey: - "Yes."

Hayward: -" You had great respect for him."

Mr Amey confirmed this and there followed detailed analysis of the work situation and intimate communications from his Mother. An old working connection with the London Underground was also verified.

In fact it is the attention to detail that convinces so many. How could I give such detail to a complete stranger of whom I knew nothing? Of course the knowledge was relayed by those in the Spiritual World.

GOOD PRACTICAL ADVICE

People consult Mediums for many reasons but it is also important to judge any information or advice with reason and common sense. Helen Tilley attended the same meeting and Mr Amey is her Father. He wrote to me regarding her communication. "The message to my Daughter was very accurate and meaningful in many ways. You were the first person to mention she was wishing to change direction career wise and that she is creative. She has, as you suggested, recommended studying and everything you said was relevant."

Although her message did not give personal evidence of survival, {you will note this had been given to her Father}, nevertheless the information given showed knowledge of her circumstances. More importantly it showed a measure of guidance from an outside source, that those in Spirit are aware of our circumstances and interested in our welfare.

AN INSPIRED DECISION

What sometimes inspires us to make a decision, are we really guided by those in the Spiritual World? Mrs Gladys Shaw of Northampton certainly thinks so. She is planning to write a book detailing some of her inspirational experiences. Although she had not met me before she decided to attend a demonstration of clairvoyance at Northampton Spiritualist Church.

She explains Geoffrey told me my Mother was present. He described her exactly including her expressions of speech. She wanted to say thank you for my caring role in the last few years. My Mother seemed to have a detailed knowledge of my life. She said that I was coping with the loss of my independence {including giving up my car} better than she did. She also knew about my health problems such as angina and high blood pressure and said with emphasis " keep taking the tablets."

104

Geoffrey then paused trying to take note of a calendar date, he said it was an important one for me. Finally he said, "The date is 16th June." This I must explain is my Fathers' birthday.

Towards the end of the service he came back to me: -
Hayward: -"There is a man here a printer named George."
This was my Husband. The medium then described his mild nature and correctly stated he had a succession of mini strokes followed by a massive stroke that damaged the brain stem. Finally he mentioned those he had met up with in the Spiritual World.

UPHEAVAL AND THE CANARY

That the Spirit World knows about our circumstances is demonstrated time and time again. Percy Tiller was a well-respected Spiritualist and regular member of Charminster Road Spiritualist Church. In 1978 he obtained evidence from his Mother who certainly knew everything that was going on.

The message started with a detailed description of his Mother that he instantly recognised. Then details of a difficult eye condition were correctly given. Then the following information: -
Hayward: - "Have you been contemplating alterations at home or are these about to be done."
Mr Tiller: - "We are doing it."
Hayward: - "You do realise the floor boards are affected and the job will take longer than originally anticipated."
Mr Tiller: - "Yes."
There followed reference to a canary in a cage that the recipient was unable to understand until he checked up after the meeting. His Mother had been totally correct. His Son had acquired a canary from a neighbour.

THE MISSING BROTHER

Sometimes sceptics impose almost impossible conditions to the criteria they would put to what they would accept as evidence. However even the toughest sceptic would be hard pressed to explain away the evidence given to Celia Atkins at a meeting in 1983 at Ringwood Spiritual Sanctuary {Hants}. The evidential message started with her Mother's name and the precise details of her passing.

105

Many years ago her Brother due to an unhappy chapter of events had left home and all contact was lost. In fact she did not know whether he was alive or dead. The message continued: -

Hayward: -"Your Mother is talking to me. I see a man in a uniform but it is not a military uniform. This man is a close relative who your Mother has a lot of interest in He is living in Bucks or Berks, the uniform looks like a Post Office uniform."

Mrs Atkins was puzzled for her Brother had been in a profession before his disappearance. However as she was anxious to trace her Brother and the rest of the message was correct she and her Husband followed the matter up. Through the information given she traced her Brother to a Post Office in Slough {Bucks} where he had been resident for five years.

INFORMATION UNKNOWN

Many times mediums are able to obtain information completely unknown by any human being. Ted Reynolds attended a meeting at Bath Road Spiritualist Church and received communication from his late Uncle Harry and his Father who he was told had a message for him.

Hayward: - "Your Father is taking me to the front of your car. He tells me there is a smell of rubber burning and also you should check the steering."

Mr Reynolds: - "I understand the details about my Father and Uncle but not about the car I will check"

Although the car was not due to have a service for at least six months he took the car into the garage. It was found on examination that the brake pads needed urgent replacement In addition the front nearside tyre was badly worn and needed immediate replacement. The recipient confirmed he had no knowledge of these faults at the time.

A SPANISH LINK

When Mrs Maria Lopez attended a demonstration of clairvoyance at the SAGB she was surprised at the private information given by the Medium who could have had no knowledge of her private circumstances.

Hayward: - "You come from Spain".

Mrs Lopez: - "Yes".

Hayward: - " Your Mother is in the Spiritual World and is with me. Before she died she suffered from heart problems. She had a great love of her home."

Mrs Lopez: - "That is all correct".

Hayward: - "Your Father is also here. He was completely different and was rarely at home"

Mrs Lopez: - "Yes "

Hayward: - "Your parents talk about La Coruna. "
Mrs Lopez: - "They were born there."
Hayward: - "They send love to your three Brothers, Alphonso and Joseph are teachers. Your third brother {here the medium got frustrated} I cannot get his name but he is a teaching priest".
Mrs Lopez: - "That is perfectly true, all of it".

AN AMERICAN COUPLES EVIDENCE

Truly the gifts of the Spirit are universal; a couple from the United States of America had sittings at the SAGB. Mrs Jacqui Doerge, although she was very nervous, was immediately put at ease. She explained "Mr Hayward did not want me to talk but wanted to tell me everything. He told me correctly about my Husband and the family unit. Then he accurately described my home and said he liked the colours and the arrangement of the furniture. He told me I wanted to work professionally and that I did not think I was good enough. As I am an oil painter and appreciate colour this was so true and I never have enough confidence.

Then details of my Grandmother Mothers side was given. He correctly stated that she had not been around to provide for the family she died when my Mother was three. He then went on to give personal details about my Daughter. He was beginning to wrap up the session and then he suddenly said": -
Hayward: - "Your Father is here he passed over so abruptly."
"That was correct, as of course were other details too personal to relate. I cannot thank Mr Hayward enough for the pure joy his sitting gave me. My Husband also had an equally evidential sitting full of personal details and descriptions." Such are the results with experienced sitters with positive attitudes.

A FATHER COMMUNICATES

It is sometimes the small minor things communicated that give a human sentimental feel to our spiritual communications. Frau Sylvia Rossburg takes a deep interest in Spiritual matters, so much so she organises Mediums to visit Hamburg in Germany to spread the good news of mankind's survival of death. She writes "I attended a meeting at the SAGB and was so impressed by Geoffrey Hayward's work and personality I invited him to Hamburg. During the course of his successful visit knowing little of my personal circumstances he gave me a sitting.

My Father communicated very strongly giving relevant details of his life, personality and details of his passing. He also showed considerable knowledge of my individual situation and that of my immediate Family. Sometimes in a message it is the small trivial things that are so evidential. It was typical of him to mention a

107

kitchen drawer that had been broken just a few days previously. Needless to say all this was completely unknown to the Medium."

A VETERANS EVIDENCE

Ken Meynell DSNU is a senior Spiritualist well respected in the movement. For many years he was associated with Parkstone Spiritualist Church. Attending a demonstration at this Centre in May 1974, he reported as follows "Your mediumship was certainly true on target as far as I was concerned, the description and all the facts were completely accurate. It was rather like someone describing my Father to me who had met him once or twice and was not quite sure who he was, it was that accurate." In the course of my career I have given tens of thousands of similar descriptions of those seen with my Spiritual vision, the vast majority of which are immediately recognised.

A MEDIUM'S HUSBAND RETURNS

Even Mediums sometimes need reassurance that their loved ones are around them and have made the adjustment to the spiritual world successfully. Vickie Hindhaugh herself a very respected and well-known Medium was not brought up a Spiritualist.. She arrived to work at the Spiritualist Association of Great Britain for the first time one day in February 1992. Certainly no one there knew of her personal circumstances. She explained "After depositing my luggage I decided to attend a demonstration of clairvoyance taken by Geoffrey Hayward who at that time I had never met. He had no way of knowing either who I was or my personal circumstances. He came to me with the following message: -
Hayward: - "I have a man here, a sailor playing a hornpipe, he tells me he is your Father."
Mrs Hindhaugh: - "Yes that is correct".
Hayward: - " I also see another man he is telling me he is George William he sings happy birthday."
Mrs Hindhaugh: - "That is my Husband, it is his birthday today."
Hayward: - "Your Husband drove buses."
Mrs Hindhaugh: - "Yes".
Hayward: - " Your Husband shows me yellow roses they are a special sign, Who was the clippy."
Mrs Hindhaugh: - "I was, we met whilst we were on the buses the yellow roses are very special."
It gave great satisfaction to give such a meaningful message to such a dedicated and sincere worker for the Spiritualist cause.

A PUZZLING MESSAGE

Another sitter who received a communication at first not understood but that on investigation turned out to be accurate was David Evans of Acton, London. Attending a public demonstration at the Spiritualist Association of Great Britain he was able to fully accept the early part of his message appertaining to his childhood.
Hayward: -"When you were a boy you spent a lot of time on a farm, what fun and adventures you got up to."
Mr Evans: - "That is perfectly true."
Hayward: - "There has been a problem with a bank."
Mr Evans: - "There has been a dispute."
Hayward: - "There has been a problem with bank charges specifically with ------ Bank."
Mr Evans: - "I cannot understand that."
Afterwards Mr Evans realised what was being referred to. There had been a serious misunderstanding with a friends bank over a money transaction that he had been involved with. The bank involved was ------.

PRIVATE COMMUNICATIONS

Sometimes one Medium will confirm information of a very personal nature that another Medium has given. Take the experience related by Sue Saunders of Bournemouth. She wrote: - "I had never been to a Medium until my Son died three years ago. Within a few weeks of his death my Sister went to see a clairvoyant. She was astounded when the only person who came through was my Son. When my Sister told me about this I was determined to see a Medium myself. I told my Son if he could communicate to show me a heart. Finally I felt ready to go to a medium. I told him nothing about myself. He immediately told me I had lost a child and this was a Son. He asked whether he had died of a heart complaint. When I said no, he said that is strange he is showing me a heart. As you can imagine I needed very little more convincing that this was indeed my Son. Since then I have seen several Mediums including yourself. On each occasion, although I have given no personal information, all the same people have come through from Spirit. A couple of weeks ago my Husband went to see a medium for the first time. Again our Son communicated. One thing he told his Dad was that he knew I was keeping all my things and he thought I should get rid of them. Then I came to see you.

Hayward: - "I have someone here called John he died too young and indeed, he looked young for his age. He had smooth skin and has been around your home. He is telling me he has been trying to turn your lights on and off. He is saying his room is the same, he does not think this is a good thing."

Sue said "everything was totally correct. The part about the lights was amazing. A few weeks ago the lights kept on going off for no apparent reason. We ended eating by candlelight. During the sitting you were able to tell me that my Mother had recently died, although I had given you no indication of this. Also you gave me the names of my two Sisters and a message from my Grandmother, thanking me for taking care of my Mother during the last part of her life as indeed I did. She came to live with us in an annexe on our house. Your description of the way she was during the last weeks of her life was also very accurate".

AN IMPORTANT MESSAGE FOR A SON

Many times during private sittings the most intimate facts and emotions are made known. Mr Fielding and his Son Mark attended a private sitting. The last person that he expected to communicate was his Father, thus ruling out the well worn theory that Mediums simply read the sitters mind.

Hayward: -"Your Father is here, he is telling me he has many regrets. He disappeared from your life because he found it difficult to deal with responsibility. He regrets what he did by walking out."

Mr Fielding: - " I understand but have long ago forgiven him for what he did."

Hayward: - "He is also sorry for what he did to your Brother by leaving home he let everyone including himself down."

Mr Fielding: - "Yes".

Hayward: - "Who is Peter".

Mr Fielding: - "That is my Brother."

A MUSICAL CONNECTION

Another example of the intimate details that can be communicated was given to Yvonne Jones of London, again at a private sitting at the Spiritualist Association Of Great Britain. After several relevant preliminary remarks the following details were given: -

Hayward: - "Your Grandmother is here she had two major qualities self discipline and self respect, she was a real disciplinarian, a product of her generation. She kept herself apart even from your Mother. She was a strong person and well respected. Your Grandfather was the quietest of the couple but he was happy to let your Gran wear the trousers so to speak.

Yvonne Jones: - "Yes I understand."

Hayward: - "You played the piano a lot when you were young. Spirit tells me you particularly enjoy Chopin {Concertos} and Rachmaninov. In fact you are a very musical person and music is very important to you. When you were younger you were good at dancing".
Yvonne Jones: -"I learned classical piano and particularly enjoyed playing Chopin."
There then followed details regarding romantic relationships that were highly relevant. Although the sitter has given me permission to quote from the highly personal details given I feel I should respect her privacy. I am extremely grateful to her for permission to quote the personal family details already given. I hope this gives an indication and highlights the complex and detailed facts so often given in sittings.
One thing that always puzzles me is the varying ease or difficulties that some people have with communicaton from the Spiritual World. This is illustrated by the next part of the message.
Hayward: - "I am feeling guilty because I have your Father here albeit not very strongly. He was not the best of communicators when he was here. He was a keen gardener, he passed quickly although he had been ill for some time."
Yvonne Jones: -"Yes."
Hayward: - "He mentions Harry".
Yvonne Jones: - "He is my Grandfather you mentioned earlier."
The sitting had an interesting conclusion. Although the session took place in London and I could have had no way of knowing she had any connection with Bournemouth, right at the end I said "You used to have a romantic link with a gentleman from Bournemouth". She confirmed she had a long time ago.

MUM AND DAD STILL WATCH OVER

That we are watched over was amply described to Valerie Archer at a sitting at the Spiritualist Association Of Great Britain Again the private and intimate knowledge of relationships and the indication to want improvement is clearly indicated here.
Hayward: - "Your Father is here he seems rather uncomfortable and embarrassed."
Valerie Archer: - "Yes". {In her narrative to me she explained she had a very difficult relationship with her Father, needless to say at the time of the sitting she was a complete stranger}.
Hayward: - " Your Mother is also with you from the Spiritual World . She died a long time ago, she tells me how you missed her in so many practical ways when you were in your twenties and thirties.
Valerie Archer: - "Yes." {Again I had no knowledge of the high significance of her Mother's words for she passed over when Mrs Archer was nineteen.}
Hayward: - "Mum and Dad tell me they take an interest in what you are doing. They tell me you have recently found a couple of old photographs of them and put them up. They also tell me you have recently been made redundant and have moved house."
Valerie Archer: - "All that is so true."

111

Hayward: - " They are right behind you in your efforts to improve. You are trying to re-invent yourself to improve still further. Someone else I do not know who tells me you are trying to become computer literate."

There was also much personal information on a relationship situation that was fully understood. Perhaps communication from the Spiritual World works best when there is a real need.

A SWISS CONNECTION

Having been originally invited to Switzerland on the recommendation of famous Psychic Artist Coral Polge I have returned to work particularly in Zurich many times. The Swiss have a reputation for exactness and in their investigations into Spiritual matters they are quite rightly totally thorough. Mrs Decurtins of Zurich received evidence that satisfied her beyond all doubt the reality of life after death. As well as the usual correct descriptions and character studies of those in Spirit some highly individual facts were given that would interest both the convinced Spiritualist and the sceptical researcher.

Hayward: - "Your family connections are very strong. Your Mother who has passed over is with you. She is such a strong character. She rushes in to be first to communicate she suffered from a lot of ill health but hid this from the family, she suffered in her lower regions for a long time."

Evidently Mrs Decurtins Mother was an excellent communicator for after confirmation of these details brought even more proof from not only her Mother but also her Father.

Hayward: - "It was her willpower that kept her going, she was tougher than you, and thinks you are too soft, she was always very busy a good organiser, she was not a good listener however. She tells me she heard what she wanted to hear and did not hear what she did not wish to hear. She has met up with your Father He was totally different. In his own quiet way however he was the strong one, he got his own way although people thought differently."

Mrs Decurtins was able to understand everything. Her Father then spoke of his own character and health difficulties with the same accuracy that her Mother had done. He confirmed that he had met up with Charles and Karl who turned out to be his Sister's Husbands, both of whom had passed over. The accuracy of the communication continued with correct details of one of the Sisters health situation. Although well pleased with the session, for the sitter had correctly not interrupted with the flow of information being given, she was disappointed that her Husband had not communicated. Patience is a virtue and often people come with the idea of communication with one individual. It is always best to accept who comes, be positive and await developments. This Mrs Decurtins did to be rewarded by this very personal and important message from her husband: -

Hayward: - "Your Husband is here, he was a strong quite well made man, but suffered with his breathing and because of this he was not himself towards the end of his life. He was a very private man, but you always knew where you were with him. He was always interested in the financial situation of the family. You have done something financial that safeguards or secures the future fairly recently, that he approves of." The recipient was able to understand the significance of this. As well as accurately describing the character of his two Sons other details followed typical of when a good contact is made by an experienced Medium: -

Hayward: - "Your Husband tells me that he would have hated to have been an invalid. He went so quickly but this was the way he would have chosen."

Mrs Decurtins: -"He actually said this the day before he died."

Hayward: -"Your Husband talks of Max."

Mrs Decurtins: - "He is my Brother."

A TRAGIC COMMUNICATOR

Alison Thorpe of Solihull had a sitting and received convincing evidence. Many ask what happens to a suicide when they pass over. Spiritualism teaches that they are helped and that our loving thoughts for them are helpful. However they also have the opportunity to help themselves. She explained "You described to me a young woman with a pronounced Scottish accent who was very distressed at the time of her passing. She had died between six and eight years ago. You described a tightening around the neck and that she had a lot of emotional problems before her death and in fact had been troubled since childhood. You said she took her own life as she was overwhelmed by what was happening to her. You also said I was harbouring some guilt about this. That I was blaming myself for not seeing it coming and feeling I could have done something to prevent it. You said that nothing I could have done would have prevented this from happening, which I found reassuring. You had perfectly described a friend of mine who had strangled herself by hanging six years previously..

AN UNEXPECTED COMMUNICATION

That there is an intelligence beyond ours acting behind the scenes in messages given is proved time and time again. Roy West attending the Portsmouth Temple Of Spiritualism received convincing evidence from his Wife, then followed a most interesting sequel: -

Hayward: - "Your Wife is telling me that she has met Ann. Now this Ann is not a relative but she was known to both of you. She had a similar illness to your Wife at exactly the same time as your Wife."

Mr West: - "That is correct".
Mr West confirmed that only a month previously he had wondered what had happened to Ann as after his Wife had passed over they had lost touch He made enquires and found out she had died a year ago. It seems Mr West's Wife had been aware of his actions.

A SON REMEMBERS

Those investigating this method of communication are perfectly entitled to get accurate information. It cannot be demanded but usually with patience it comes. Mr and Mrs Whitlock had a sitting at the Glasgow Association of Spiritualists. Here is their experience: -
Hayward: - "You have lost a Son, he went quickly he was almost catapulted into the spirit world."
Mr& Mrs Whitlock: -"Yes."
Hayward: - "Is there a Doug or a Douglas the only other thing I keep getting did he or you have any connection with Sinclair."
Mr & Mrs Whitlock: - "The accident occurred on the corner of Douglas Drive and Sinclair Street ask him whether Fudge is with him."
Hayward: - "I am not getting Fudge he is talking about a sandpit, he is very happy in a sandpit, you cannot get him out of it."
Mr & Mrs Whitlock: - "That is true."
Hayward: -"No Fudge is a little bit of a question mark, is Fudge a dog? I am getting a dog like a Golden Retriever".
Mr & Mrs Whitlock: -"Fudge was a Golden Labrador."

MESSAGES OF CONFIRMATION

The Spiritual World has many ingenious ways of proving their presence. Fred and Pauline Poole were regular members of my developing circle. Fred writes " One of the many outstanding pieces of evidence came two days after reading in the local paper that an old colleague had passed. It was not until I read this that I discovered that George had a hyphenated surname. I only knew him by the second part of his full name. So I was more than a little surprised when you gave me a message from him using the first part of his surname"

A FATHER'S REFLECTION

114

Mr Napier of Kingsbury like many before him was helped therapeutically by the messages he received. Sitting at the SAGB he explained that his relationship with his Father was difficult. He went on to explain that firstly his Grandfather communicated and brought his Father in. His Father immediately correctly said that he passed over very quickly. He then indicated that he had failed to show commitment to his Son and there was a lack of understanding on his part. He now realises he should have done better. A lot of other intimate details were given convincing the sitter how much the Father was watching over and helping him. In fact such was the impact that he looks upon his relationship with his Father much more positively.

A CAREER GUIDED BY SPIRIT

Mediumship sometimes poses more questions than it answers. Taking a packed meeting at the SAGB, renowned Psychic Artist Coral Polge was drawing the portraits and Geoffrey Hayward was connecting in clairvoyantly. Mrs Garg was in the audience, her Daughter who was not present at the meeting was studying at medical school, her exams only being a few days away .She witnessed the following: -
Hayward: -"I have a message for a medical student" {there followed a detailed description of the surroundings of the university building and also a clock tower}.
Mrs Garg: - "I think you may be with me my Daughter she is a medical student."
Hayward: - "The gentleman Coral is drawing is an Austrian eye specialist".
Coral Polge: - "Yes I agree with that, he dates from the 1800s, he is guiding your Daughter."
Hayward: - "Yes and he is guiding her with her studies, there are some important examinations coming up."
Mrs Garg: - "Yes".
Hayward: - "Your Daughter needs to concentrate on the subject of eyes as these will come up in the examination."

Many such messages are given week in week out by the many excellent Mediums who work in our societies and churches. No one but the recipient can hope to evaluate the impact or accuracy of the communication. In this particular case Mrs Garg passed on the message to her Daughter. She took the advice and particularly concentrated on the study of the eye as recommended. Although the examination covered a very wide field on all sorts of medical topics the specific topic of the eye came up as predicted. Mrs Garg's Daughter Monica was suitably impressed with the helpful advice regarding the examination topic that helped her to pass. In addition the university grounds were just as described, she spent her lunchtimes in the grounds under a clock tower!

A HAPPY PREDICTION

Can Mediums predict the future, should Mediums prophesy this is certainly a controversial subject? No medium, of course, should revert to fortune telling. However it seems those in the Spiritual World know something of the likely pathway ahead. Certainly it is a mediums job to relay accurately and honestly that given. Mrs Prentice of Bournemouth was given a highly interesting message concerning the future.

Hayward: - "Your Daughter will meet her future Husband on the 14th March. Your Mother tells me this, she also says not to tell your Daughter about this message, until after it has happened. Mother also tells me she will have two Sons and a Daughter The two Sons will be named Jack and David again you must not say about this."

Although at this time her Daughter was in a long-term relationship it transpired that this relationship ended and she did indeed meet the man she married on the date predicted. Happily they have two Sons named Conor JACK and Callum DAVID. At the time of writing she is expecting again.

A PROMISE FULFILLED

Audrey and Kim Reynolds received a promise from their Mother that she would attempt to communicate after she passed over. Audrey writes, "following the death of our Mother, my Brother and I decided to seek the assistance of a Spiritualist Medium to contact her. We contacted the local Spiritualist church that highly recommended Geoffrey Hayward. At this point we were highly sceptical but with trepidation we made an appointment. When we called, Geoff made it quite clear that he did not want any details about his sitters, not their names or whom they wanted to contact. Our first sitting with Geoff was hard to describe. He immediately told us that our Mother had passed and was with us in the room. He said although she had only recently passed she wanted to fulfil her promise to let us know that she was ok. The details given about her illness and subsequent death and even the most intimate character details were astounding. Not only Mum's character but the personalities of other family members and how her death was effecting them. Geoff described other family members that were with her who we did not recognise at the time. The specific names and descriptions were identified as our Grandmother and Mum's Sister both of whom died at a young age and we had never met.

A BROTHER REMEMBERS

As often mentioned it is the small trivial things that are sometimes evidential. Ulla Hochst attended a meeting at the Lichtquelle Spiritual Centre near Dortmund. After giving a description of her Brother I said: -

Hayward: - "Your Brother thanks you very much for lighting the candles for him. A few days ago you lit a large number of candles for a most special occasion, he was very touched by this."

Ulla Hochst: - " Yes I did it was for his anniversary,"

Sometimes a few simple words mean so much.

LOOK NO TIE

Sylvie Votta had a sitting and one of the messages she received had a particular significance.

Her Father had passed on six years before while in Spain, where he had been living, Sylvie being there at the time. He always dressed very smartly, even in the heat of Spain he would never go out without a jacket and tie, as he said he would not feel dressed! Sylvie tried on many occasions to get him to lighten up, even buying him smart casual shirts, to no avail. At the sitting he was standing next to her, with a big beaming smile and a good tan, the message he gave (with his big hearty laugh) was to tell her he was not wearing a tie!

This message meant a lot to Sylvie lifting her heart and confirming he is always there with her.

A SCEPTIC CONVINCED

Translation of letter from Silke Lorenz regarding her first experience of contact.

I was very sceptical going to the public demonstration having contact with the dead by the British Medium Geoffrey Hayward!

I was interested of course. Especially because I lost a very good friend recently in a motorbike accident. His death left me with two main questions, which I was thinking about during the trip from home to Hagen.

1. Did he suffer or was he dead straight away? He fell in the Alps and they did not know whether he broke his neck straight away on a stone or whether he lived through the fall.

2. Obviously he drove too fast. Why did he do that? Why did he play with his life? Or were there other circumstances that caused the accident?

I had a friend with me in the car and while driving we were talking about our scepticism. Of course we thought that there would be people in the audience that the

Medium knew. So he would talk to them and they would confirm whatever he was saying. We thought that these people would sit there to convince the rest of the congregation that contact with the dead is possible.

But what I experienced at the public demonstration convinced me totally!

At first Geoffrey had contact for some men and women in the group. That was not surprising for me because I kind of expected that anyway.

Then he had a message for my friend from her Father. What he said was true. He even gave his first name and name of his Wife. At this stage I got really nervous. Some time later Geoffrey turned to me and asked: "Who is the young gentleman that died in a motorbike accident belonging to?"

I said: "He might belong to me!" Now I think that almost every person knows somebody that died in a motorbike accident and of course those people are mainly young men!

But then this... Geoffrey said: "He asks me to tell you that he did not suffer. His neck was broken straight away! And it was not his fault. These are the two questions that you came here to get the answers. He was cremated after he died. He died just before a bend in the road."

All this information is correct!

And then this: "He is not where you keep on looking for him. He is with you. He is here now. He is come with a lot of love for you. He thanks you for your love, your thoughts and your prayers. You do not have to go to places to find him. He is not there. He is with you anyway." I must admit that I go to the cemetery regularly. I have only been there a few days ago, although his grave is about 100 kilometres away from where I live. And I went to the Alps to where he crashed. I had to go there to say goodbye to him.

And because my friend knows how sceptical I am he added the following information:

"Every morning he laughs a lot about you! Because you are always in a rush. You fly out of bed and you leave chaos of sheets and quilts. (I use three quilts at the moment!) I could not stand upright in your flat. There must be a low ceiling or something there. (That is correct he couldn't stand up in my flat.)

"Who is Willi?" (My Sister's dog, that I just played with before I came here!)

"Willi is a very small dog and he always eats the wrong things!"

(He's a Yorkshire and is regularly sick on the floor because of this!)

"Whose birthday is in April?" (My Sister's and my Husband's.)

Geoffrey decided that he wanted my Sister. He asked if my friend knew my Sister. I said no but Geoffrey insisted that there must be something between him and my Sister. And yes it was a running joke between him and me. As he was single and lonely, looking for a partner he kept asking me if I had a Sister. And he asked every time we spoke or saw each other. He said: "Silki don't you have a Sister?" Each time I said: "Yes, but you know that she is married."

Where should Geoffrey get this information from if not from my friend?

Another thing I noticed while I saw Geoffrey work is that he changed energetically with each message. With old people from spirit he spoke slowly, he was calm, stern or funny. But when I got the message from my friend Geoffrey seemed very vital, lively and dynamic almost excited. Like my friend when he was alive: a power pack. Geoffrey kept on coming back to me: "He is with you with a lot of love." That is also very typical for my friend, like hey I am still here and I have got to say something.

When I went back home in the car I turned the music on and the first lines I heard were:
"Every breath you take... I'll be watching you."
Coincidence? I don't think so!
At home I rang my friend's Brother and told him what I had experienced. Some days later he called me and asked: "Did he really say that he is not where we are looking for him?" Then he told me that the priest gave a bible quote to his Mother after the cremation: "I am not where you are looking for me." This information I did not even have myself.

Since that evening with Geoffrey I am feeling much better. The torturing questions have gone and I can feel that my friend is with me. It is good to think that I only have to say goodbye to his body but I know that we are kindred spirits and that we will never be alone.

If on reading this book any of my sitters have had communications of a similar evidential nature and would like these included in a later edition please let me know. In the years ahead I believe much research will be made into psychic gifts and Spirituality. Already people are starting to value the use of meditation and the development of the human psyche. Dear fellow searchers after truth I seek to show you the way just as others have shown me this spiritual pathway I hope my epitaph will be that I will leave this Earth a little better for my presence here.

One day a lady was talking to me. She said "Mr Hayward you must meditate to some wonderfully spiritually inspired music" .I answered "Madam I always meditate to the rock band Dire Straits." Always keep your feet on the floor and always remember this life is for living and finding the balance between the spiritual and material.

CONCLUSIONS

The evidence described in this book and the similar evidence obtained by countless others investigating this subject cannot be explained away by telepathy or the lost memory recalled. The exact description of a personality, the colour of a favourite dress, the peculiar layout of a room. This proves the individual spirit goes on. The anniversary correctly dated, the certain song recalled, the individuals mannerisms of speech. All these things will be recalled to every investigator. All that is needed is patience and an open mind. Those who think the messages are too trivial should stop to consider certain things. Those in the spirit world attempting this method of communication once lived here on Earth. In this life much of our communication is made up of discussing seemingly insignificant things of little importance to the outsider.

The question of telepathy is an important one. The work of Soviet researchers {already explained} was for the purpose of espionage rather than for spiritual reasons. Despite painstaking research the wavelength {perhaps fortunately} have never been found. So every effort to find a material explanation for telepathy have been unsuccessful. Yet practically everyone experiences telepathic communication fairly frequently in their lives. Spiritualists are not afraid to admit the reality of telepathy. I fully accept the communication between my spiritual self and those in the Spiritual World is a telepathic one. Surely it is logical to accept there is telepathy between the living and the so called dead as well as telepathy between us here on Earth. We must be careful not to confuse the mind with the brain. The brain is physical whilst the mind is not. Now if mental mediumship was merely the medium picking thoughts up from the sitter's mind we would always get the communication we were expecting. Not only that but there are frequent examples where the communications show an intellect of their own. In addition there are numerous instances when those in the Spiritual World have given facts completely unknown or totally opposite of the sitters knowledge that has on investigation turned out completely correct. Whenever I have tried so called telepathy tests I have constantly scored below chance expectation. If my gifts were really just telepathic thoughts picked from the sitters mind I would make a highly successful living in the cabaret circuit and be considerably more wealthy than I am now!

In this life many people only seek fame, wealth, influence, prestige. Their values of acclamation, abundance, power and powerful reputation can in itself give no spiritual satisfaction. So therefore many are looking for other things more meaningful and lasting to obtain peace of mind and security. So an awareness of our spiritual selves through the study and investigation of the phenomena and philosophy that Spiritualism has to offer broadens our horizons and spiritual awareness.

My spiritual vision and insight does not come from mystical, secret or ascetic practices . You cannot develop into a medium by solely receiving esoteric teachings or attending expensive meditation courses. If you have the gift within you {although most cannot develop to a professional standard the majority can considerably increase their spiritual insight} how can you develop? The simple answer is through good balanced living and the desire to use your gifts to help others. In other words development of your inner spirit within.

The phenomena of Spiritualism would however mean nothing without an accompanying philosophy. Much progress has been made in recent years. Despite continued opposition from vested interests, much of the derision and contempt of former times have gone. Spiritualism helps us to understand more of the human consciousness and the existence not only of the unlimited powers around us but of a Spiritual World and a spiritual universe. Of course there is much work still to be done. Spiritualism teaches us we must reassess our outlook on life. Surely therefore the philosophical implications of the reality of the spiritual world around us is that mankind places a greater value upon spiritual things. This is difficult, as many have been brought up to believe in our existence from a purely material standpoint. As a Spiritualist I believe this is not a true or final standard of valuation. The reality of the psychic gifts and psychic phenomena so constantly demonstrated in this book also involves us with a re-evaluation of our personality and makeup. Through my own gifts and spiritual search I have tried to extend my insight and knowledge to deal with my own restrictions and struggles. Surely my spiritual knowledge should improve my personal relationships with those around me as well as my relationship with the material and physical world around us.

I make no excuses for bringing analytical study into this. Although I have quoted from one or two classical cases of spiritual communication, my object has been to present in a detailed way new cases never before published giving evidence of the spiritual nature of us and of existence of a spiritual life beyond this. But we cannot underestimate the philosophical and practical implications of this here and now. Spiritualism unlike so many philosophies is about the individual and the search for self-identity. In other words although the acceptance of the reality of communication and of survival is vitally important this in itself is not enough. Perhaps it is the reluctance of even some attached to the Spiritualist movement to recognise the true philosophical implications that has meant the movement has not made the progress, given the rich spiritual content of its true nature. Certainly at the moment there are too many other philosophies creeping into our churches and societies.

In my view at the end of the day everything comes down to evidence. Spiritualism is not a blind belief but stands for certain established facts. Of course throughout history there have been stories handed down from every age and civilisation of psychic happenings. Although the modern Spiritualist would accept that some of these stories are nothing more than myths with little foundation in truth others are similar to those experienced by countless people today. We realise the psychic or intuitive part of us is a very natural part of us. It follows that the understanding and cultivation of these gifts is desirable to understand our true selves. This pathway as we have seen I have followed for many years. Although many times this chosen route has been hard it has been a rich journey of self-discovery that I urge you to follow.

Life is uncertain and as a Spiritualist I certainly do not bury my head in the sand. The true appeal of Spiritualist philosophy is that it has a modern approach to modern problems. Life does have a design and purpose that is spiritual in content. Whilst I accept through my long struggle dealing with my own sensitivity {and my school days when I was bullied and other times when I have felt so much the outsider particularly come to mind} was difficult it helped to forge my spiritual identity. It is not easy to penetrate into our spiritual inner selves. Many drug addicts start out to quicken this awareness. Such actions are VERY DANGEROUS as drugs lower the moral and mental character principles and inner strength of the individual. I am not saying a true knowledge of our spiritual make up would eradicate our drug problem but it would help. So we need to re-educate as to our spiritual responsibilities and destiny.

Spiritualism does teach the value of meditation that is in essence communion with the inner self. In seeking the quietness of listening to our inner selves. The need to meditate in this ever more demanding world is greater than ever. In meditation it is important to forget our physical selves and physical restrictions. To truly relax and commune with your inner being.

In my work as a medium without the aid of those from the Spiritual World I am nothing,my work is not about converting anyone. Although I have written mainly of my spiritual work I have also made you aware of my other interests including my political philosophy. Again the conclusions I have reached are highly personal and individual to me. My truth is my truth due to my individual experiences. Your truth is your truth that you hold equally dear. I defend your right to defend your truth just as much as I defend mine. There are those who say contact with the Spiritual world is not desirable and the subject should be left alone. Although that is not my view nevertheless so be it. My experience is that from a very early age I had this gift whether I wanted it or not. Rather than run away from it I made using my free will to consciously develop that within me hopefully to benefit others. Since that time I have not had a moments regret. I have been blessed and protected by those in the spirit around me. There is sometimes loose talk of the influence of so called bad spirits, those of low moral character. Obviously there must be danger of this in uncontrolled conditions but again I can only speak from my personal experience. In all the thousands of messages that I have given in thirty years work I have only heard words of concern and loving kindness from those in spirit directing us to conduct ourselves with dignity and respect. In fact I believe that this contact also helps them on their spiritual progress.

The subject of free will is an interesting one that will be continuously debated. It is closely connected with the question whether Mediums are able toforetell future events. If we accept precognition we must accept that human action can be foreseen. It raises all sorts of questions to the enquiring mind. I do not consider enough research has been done, within the Spiritualist movement let alone outside of it, regarding the true nature of the psychic capacity of the mind.

The Victorian psychic researcher Frank Podmore, after many years research came to the conclusion that he could find no evidence that would or could convince him of survival. Most modern researchers would disagree with this attitude of mind. I hope this book has been helpful to the researcher,the newcomer the convinced Spiritualist and the sceptic and that together we should move forward to find the spiritual purpose to life and living.

I am convinced that many have an erroneous view of the true nature of Spiritualism. Also many old superstitions remain about contact with the Spiritual World around us. This book has not been about the conditions and realities that we will one day experience in the Spirit World.that world of wider reality. I am sure we will all face individual trial and tribulations when we reach there. I have never thought that the Spirit World is " Disneyland" in the sky. But I do know that we will take with us, not our material possessions or fancy titles. We will take our character and our memories to that other world. However the average man and woman has nothing to fear from passing from this life to the next stage of existence.

The philosophy of Spiritualism teaches us that psychic or spiritual experiences are nothing to fear. In fact they are both natural and desirable. It shows our intuitional perceptions are real and tangible. It brings new standards, values and stimulus into our lives. As an Astronomer I am aware that they ridiculed Copernicus and Galileo for stating the Earth went round the Sun. The discoveries they made changed mankind's view of not only the universe but of themselves. They forced the scientific conventions of their time to change and adapt. In our own time science has movable boundaries and definitions. The scientific community has been forced to accept many of the truths propagated by Spiritualists for years. Too many people living with indoctrinated materialistic ideas that stifle real growth define this age. We clearly see this in the World around us. The truths of Spiritualism showing the true spiritual nature of man attempts to bring a new meaning to our lives.

This book has been more about life and trying to find a greater meaning to our existence here. As well as proving the reality of a Spiritual World around us accessible to all who care to investigate with an open and honest mind. I hope the reader will have been comforted, consoled, inspired and motivated to start, continue or enhance their knowledge of this very fascinating subject. To come to the same conclusions of many of us. Not only of the Spiritual purpose of life but of the fact that communication with the Spiritual World is both desirable and possible. **THAT TRULY THERE IS NO DEATH.**